# The Large Church

p 47 -
Wesley put
1 in 10
1 in 5 to work with
significant leadership -
& ministry - common people
ready to serve!

community became the incubator
& training camp for Christ like
ministry -

# The Large Church

### A Twentieth-Century Expression
### of the First-Century Church

## JOHN N. VAUGHAN

**BAKER BOOK HOUSE**
Grand Rapids, Michigan 49506

Library of Congress
Catalog Card Number: 84-73377

ISBN: 0-8010-9298-1

Printed in the United States of America

To my mother and father
in appreciation

# Contents

# *Foreword*

Unlike other books, this book represents original research which clearly makes a new contribution to the field of church growth. This research on the role of the small groups as they are used by the large church will be helpful to the theoreticians and practitioners alike.

The historical section is of particular interest. Tracing the size of churches and their sanctuaries through periods of Christian history is fascinating. This is the first time it has been done in church growth literature to my knowledge. It whets the appetite for more. Further research along these lines could be significant for the field of American and world church growth.

The focus of this book is the unique role of how the large church has had a definite place in church history. An urban world like ours today needs to be reminded of this unique role of the large church in proclaiming the gospel of Jesus Christ to millions who have not heard. The large church, through use of small groups, has proven to be uniquely able to be used by the Holy Spirit in our times. People in the small groups minister to each other in ways that they would ordinarily not; within only the large church they are not able to become acquainted with individual needs and problems except in the small groups. And knowing they are all a part of the larger church gives each person a feeling of being a part of an ongoing work of God.

I heartily recommend this book to all pastors and church leaders who are prayerfully seeking for key guidelines for church growth.

*Paul Yonggi Cho*
Senior Pastor
Yoido Full Gospel Church
Seoul, Korea

# Introduction

The decade of the 1960s is remembered as an era in American church history when the institutional church was unpopular. Critics attempted to direct public attention to the rising importance of small home groups popularized through the "underground church."

Then, in the 1970s there was a shift to an almost unapologetic boldness in the building of large churches. With this commitment to growth, the number of churches with 2,000 people attending each week increased from a mere dozen to more than a hundred by 1984. Reports also began to appear announcing the existence of even larger churches beyond the borders of the United States.

Today, during the 1980s, frequent reports identify the activities of megachurches with weekly attendance exceeding 5,000 people. This rapid growth of large churches around the world has aroused renewed interest in the large churches of the past, present, and future. Several assumptions about growing churches are surveyed in the following pages. Let it be understood from the beginning of our study that big is not necessarily better in all situations, any more than small is better. God appears to use churches of all sizes to accomplish his specific purposes in his master plan of worldwide dominion.

## Assumptions about Church Growth

*Every church begins small and most remain small.* Churches seldom grow large enough to have 350 people in attendance. Donald A. McGavran, dean emeritus of the School of World Mission and Institute of Church Growth at Fuller Theological Seminary, comments,

> Everything starts small. We must not say smallness is a sign of failure.... To some He has given one talent, and to some He has given ten.... It is not helpful to think of bigness as a mark of success, and smallness as a mark of failure. We must also look at the situation....[1]

> You cannot love people and support them in their needs ... unless you know them. Large churches must have many small compartments, churches within churches, so to speak to be effective.[2]

The large congregation is chosen for this study because of its unequaled potential for influencing small churches and a city for God. Many people make the mistake of assuming that the large church is merely an enlarged small church. This assumption has serious implications and is often believed by those who lead both large and small churches.

*Time brings transition to every congregation.* Every large church will someday be smaller and any small church may someday be larger. Frequent observation of listings of large churches reveals that eventually time brings transition in each congregation. Eventually all large congregations are displaced by other more rapidly growing churches.

The chronicles of North America's growing churches provide evidence of this assertion. During the three decades from 1949 to 1979 three different churches were ranked as the nation's largest (see table 1). From 1949 to 1979, attendance at First Baptist Church of Fort Worth declined from 5,200 to about 500. During the period 1959 to 1979, First Baptist Church of Hammond grew from 800 to 15,101.

Although some congregations are able to have sustained growth for periods exceeding those of others around them, the message becomes obvious that every church is only one generation from either numerical increase or decline. Every generation is accountable for its own hour of opportunity to win and reach the multitudes at its doors.

Elmer L. Towns speaks to the issue of the vision and boldness of the

1. Donald A. McGavran with Win C. Arn, *How to Grow a Church* (Glendale, Calif.: Regal, 1973), p. 70.
2. Ibid., p. 72.

Table 1  **The Largest Churches, 1949–1979**

|  | Year | Sunday-School Attendance |
|---|---|---|
| *First Baptist Church Fort Worth, Texas* | 1949 | 5,200 |
| *Akron Baptist Temple Akron, Ohio* | 1969 | 5,762 |
| *First Baptist Church Hammond, Indiana* | 1979 | 15,101 |

Statistics are from Louis Entzminger, *How to Organize and Administer a Great Sunday School* (Fort Worth: The Manning Company, 1949), p. iii; Elmer L. Towns, *The Ten Largest Sunday Schools and What Makes Them Grow* (Grand Rapids: Baker, 1969), pp. 154–55; and Elmer L. Towns, John N. Vaughan, and David J. Seifert, *The Complete Book of Church Growth* (Wheaton: Tyndale House, 1981), p. 356.

church's heart: "The super-aggressive church is large in the heart of the leader long before it expands on the street corner."[3]

*Large churches tend to affect rather than be affected by national institutional influences.* Unlike smaller churches that often depend on other congregations, small and large, for community strength, the large church often functions as a denomination itself. Large churches tend to affect national denominational policy, whereas the smaller churches tend to reflect denominational policy.

*Large churches tend to function paradoxically and simultaneously as minidenominations and macrocosms of small groups.* These two traits offer a clue to the greatest hope of survival for the large church during times of widespread economic crisis. During good times the large organization offers a broad umbrella of hope that extends over its territorial domain. During hard times several options are open as small-group strategy is intensified.

These options are to be found in the current variety of small-group structural strategies in large churches both in the United States and in other countries. Research of these strategies and their growth climates now will insure more effective adaptation in similar large churches during times of transition and crisis.

*Many smaller churches may best learn small-group growth principles from the large churches.* Size is an issue that is debated by critics from the ranks of small churches. Seldom do leaders or supporters of large churches criticize themselves. But because most criticisms come from

3. Elmer L. Towns, *Is the Day of the Denomination Dead?* (Nashville: Nelson, 1973), p. 134.

small churches, they reflect criticisms of large churches learned in their past.

Volumes have been written about the uniqueness of both large and small churches. Despite the uniqueness of each, for the kingdom's sake, both can and must learn principles of church growth from one another. Large churches appear to be doing better at this task than are the smaller churches.

Charles L. Chaney shares his alertness about how small and large churches complement one another: "Generally, the smaller the church, the higher the baptismal rate. However, churches with more than 3,000 members are more evangelistically effective than churches with 500–2,999 members."[4]

*Planting of new churches by parent congregations predates denominational church planting.* Churches, from early New Testament times (Acts 11:19–13:52), have been entrusted with the responsibility for planting other churches.[5] Throughout church history parachurch groups have assumed and on occasion have been assigned the task of church planting. Although God has honored both methods, the responsibility of the church has not been nullified, although it has been abdicated on occasion.

*The rate of planting new congregations influences the rate at which large segments of the unchurched are being reached by congregations.*

*Satellite groups owned and operated by many large churches are functionally the same although different in polity from new churches planted by more traditional methods.* Traditional church planting in the United States usually creates fewer than two or three mission or satellite churches at the same time. Most new churches also are intended to become autonomous churches soon after they are planted.

However, mission or satellite groups administered by several of the world's larger churches vary widely in structure and may or may not become autonomous once they are planted. Baptists and other groups governed by more congregationally oriented views of church government have great difficulty with this modified episcopal and sometimes presbyterial structure. Congregations with a European church-state heritage have much less difficulty.

4. Charles L. Chaney, *Church Planting at the End of the Twentieth Century* (Wheaton: Tyndale House, 1982), p. 160.

5. Floyd G. Bartel and Richard Showalter, *A New Look at Church Growth* (Newton, Kans.: Faith and Life Press; Scottdale, Penn.: Mennonite Publishing House, 1979), p. 97.

Alfred Kuen, a European advocate of the Free church structure, quotes one pastor who summarizes the basic difference simply but clearly. He views the episcopal form as placing priority on the whole rather than the parts. Congregational groups, however, place a first priority on the parts, with the whole being secondary.[6]

The priesthood of the former is more institutional, whereas the focus of the latter is more on the priesthood of the believer. Both increase memberships—the former through specific territory (e.g., a parish) and the other by voluntary association and statement of conversion.

## The Scope of This Study

The issues of satellite-group ministries in many of the world's largest congregations center around questions of scriptural and historical validity and definition of the terms *church*, *denomination*, and *parachurch*. Other issues include priesthood of the believer, autonomy of local congregations, and optimum size of Christian congregations.

Large congregations differ from smaller ones in various ways. We will specifically consider how the larger units are uniquely able to create several satellite congregations or a network of cell groups of a dozen people each in members' homes. This capability to generate multiple groups is a key trait of the large church. Small satellite groups radiate from a parent church rather than as isolated autonomous congregations.

A brief introduction to large Jewish synagogues in the New Testament world is given as background to early church building by Christian communities.

An overview of the construction of Christian worship structures is presented to establish the long history of large assembly centers used by Christians. Once discussion is completed about the first four centuries of the Christian era, exclusive attention is focused on Free churches in the Protestant tradition. This study includes both independent and denominational congregations.

Omitted from consideration are cathedrals and Roman Catholic worship centers like the 22,000-seat basilica dedicated by Cardinal Roncalli, who subsequently became Pope John XXIII. Located in Lourdes, France, it is reported to receive more than 500,000 pilgrims

---

6. Alfred Kuen, *I Will Build My Church*, trans. Ruby Lindblad (Chicago: Moody, 1971), p. 238.

annually. The basilica is an enclosure for religious services and not a church in the ordinary sense of the word.[7]

## The Purpose of This Study

The intent of this study is to examine the large congregation in early and recent church history. Early church buildings and records give clues as to how Christians worshiped. Later buildings and records are helpful in understanding how large churches have increasingly returned to the New Testament mandate to become centers of church planting for world evangelization.

Contemporary large congregations using satellite groups of varied design are considered valid models, for they take seriously their responsibility as centers for evangelism to their own metropolitan area. Other models, mostly in Latin America, are omitted here because they extend their ministries hundreds of miles across state and national lines.

One hopes that churches, small and large, will be informed, encouraged, and challenged to recognize how large, growing churches continue to expand in size, social influence, and evangelism through the effective use of small groups. For our purposes, a small group should be understood to be a group with no fewer than five and no more than thirty people. In most instances it is understood to refer to a group of five to twenty-five people.

## The Methodology of This Study

### Personal Experience

Both small and large churches have been an important part of my own life and ministry. My parents took me to a growing congregation with attendance exceeding 1,000 each week. During and following seminary, I have served in two congregations exceeding 3,000 members and another with more than 5,000 members. Two of these churches were actively involved in television ministries that extended their outreach to the greater metropolitan area. I have served in churches ranging from 5 to 5,000 members.

Interest in other large churches has led me to visit most of the largest

7. G. E. Kidder, *The New Churches of Europe* (London: The Architectural Press, 1964), p. 110.

churches in this country. Recent visits to large churches in other countries have encouraged me in the research for this project.

Application of this interest led to the opportunity to co-author *The Complete Book of Church Growth* with Towns and David J. Seifert in 1981. Also, as follow-up of that work, research was begun for another book, *The World's Twenty Largest Churches*. Research for both of these books has introduced me to much detailed information on large churches of the world.

### Exegetical Method

Any study of Christian churches is void of any prospect of authenticity if Scripture is not consulted. The value of Scripture in this examination of the nature, structure, and function of New Testament churches is unusually critical.

*Ekklesia,* the Greek word that is the equivalent of the English word *church,* appears only three times in Matthew's Gospel. The remainder of the 115 occurrences of the Greek word are scattered from Acts to Revelation and are translated either "church" or "assembly."

Does this mean that the church was unimportant to Jesus? Why did he omit it as a major theme? Kuen offers a solution to these questions: "When Jesus wishes to reveal to His disciples truths which they were still unable to comprehend, He frequently used images and parables."[8]

Paul S. Minear, Winkley Professor of Biblical Theology at Yale Divinity School, singles out ninety-six images and parables used in the New Testament for the church and the kingdom. These images are vital in the messages they communicate about the church.[9]

### Historical Literary Analysis

Familiarity with extrabiblical literary sources from the first four centuries allows validation of some claims about the early church. This same familiarity helps the researcher to deal with unfounded, wishful thinking or misinformation from well-meaning observers.

Clement of Rome (c. 95), Ignatius (c. 115), Justin Martyr (c. 150), Tertullian (c. 150), Eusebius of Caesarea (c. 325), and John Chrysostom (c. 380) each contributed information about the early church before and during their own lifetimes. These sources also help distinguish the

8. Kuen, *I Will Build My Church*, p. 83.

9. Paul S. Minear, *Images of the Church in the New Testament* (Philadelphia: Westminster, 1960).

polity and structure of the earlier churches as being biblical or extra-biblical in character.

### Research Tools

To insure as much accuracy as possible in gathering my data on the world's twenty largest churches, I designed a questionnaire (see Appendix A). The intent was to gather data previously unavailable and to determine from it growth trends and structures of each church.

Next, a team of missionary researchers was enlisted in each of the countries where these large churches are located. Each missionary received a copy of the questionnaire to be completed during a personal interview with the pastor, a staff member, or a person chosen by the pastor to represent him. Each missionary chosen for this project knew the language and customs of the people. This proved most valuable during my visit with the pastors and leaders of the churches of Chile, Brazil, and Korea.

# 1

# *Fourteen Issues Related to Large Churches with Satellite Groups*

O ne of the few writers to voice the real issues related to the whole question of church growth by division is Howard A. Snyder.

Snyder, formerly dean of the Free Methodist Seminary in São Paulo, is currently director of Light and Life Men International. A major speaker at the 1974 International Congress on World Evangelization in Lausanne, Switzerland, he is also author of *The Problem of Wine Skins*, *The Radical Wesley and Patterns for Church Renewal*, and *The Community of the King*. His view of the church and its role in history focuses on his wrestling with difficult questions.

> Growth by division, or the multiplication of local congregations, is not a biblical principle in the same sense that Christian community life or the exercise of spiritual gifts are biblical principles. It is rather a conclusion many have reached through studying the New Testament church growth throughout history. Its biblical basis is two-fold: the analogy from physical life and the example of the early church.[1]

1. Howard A. Snyder, *The Community of the King* (Downers Grove: Inter-Varsity, 1977), pp. 128–29.

Snyder then suggests six key questions that probe the heart of the whole concept of satellite-group ministry, which fosters multiplication by division. Most of his six questions are incorporated as part of the fourteen issues.

## Universality

Will multiplication by division work anywhere at any time or is its effectiveness limited to certain geographical and social climates of the world? Snyder's answer is, "The multiplication of local cells of believers is more difficult in some cultures than in others, but it is totally impossible only under the most repressive totalitarian regimes."[2] Reports from China give cause for hope even there.

Paul Yonggi Cho, pastor of Yoido Full Gospel Church (formerly Full Gospel Central Church) in Seoul, shares his conviction about the issue: "This is evangelism. This is church growth. By the end of 1980 we had 10,000 home cell groups. I firmly believe that when any church adopts this system of home cell groups, it is going to grow."[3]

## Authority

This issue is perhaps the most debated and essential. Both critics and proponents of satellite-group organizational structure agree on the critical priority of authority, but their actual selection of authority sources often differs radically.

Jerry White, executive director of the Navigators, identifies four authority sources that can be helpful in our evaluation of church-growth structures.

> We first must determine what we will accept as our authority. Our choices are:
> 1. Scripture alone
> 2. Scripture and church history
> 3. Scripture, church history, tradition
> 4. Scripture, church history, tradition, current human authority (i.e., a pope)[4]

2. Ibid., p. 129.

3. Paul Yonggi Cho with Harold Hostetler, *Successful Home Cell Groups* (Plainfield, N.J.: Logos International, 1981), p. 64.

4. Jerry White, *The Church and the Parachurch: An Uneasy Marriage* (Portland: Multnomah, 1983), p. 63.

He then identifies most evangelicals and conservatives with the first view, with others in the same theological ranks adopting the second and third alternatives.

> As we view ... great variation in the structures of various local churches, we can become confused about what is biblical. Even within evangelical circles there is wide variation.... Most structures and forms, even in "unstructured" local congregations, are a result of tradition or current cultural choice. But they are not therefore unbiblical ... we cannot mandate our forms for everyone, or treat them as sacred.[5]

The spectrum of authority structures ranges from those groups under highly structured systems (i.e., Roman Catholics) to those who have divested themselves of all apparent authority roles (i.e., nonstructured house churches).

White proposes that authority structures can be assigned to any one of at least ten categories, from high authority to low authority:

1. Roman Catholic
2. Anglo-Catholic
3. Hierarchical (bishops, centralized authority)
4. Denominational (elder rule)
5. Denominational (congregational rule)
6. Associational (elder rule)
7. Associational (congregational rule)
8. Independent (elder rule)
9. Independent (congregational rule)
10. Nonstructured House Churches[6]

The prevailing mood seems to recognize the biblical blueprint while also acknowledging the significant role of cultural and traditional adaptations in most existing growth models. This is also the view of David J. Hesselgrave and William R. Read, Victor M. Monterroso, and Harmon A. Johnson.[7]

5. Ibid., pp. 76–77.

6. Ibid., p. 77.

7. See David J. Hesselgrave, *Planting Churches Cross-Culturally: A Guide for Home and Foreign Missions* (Grand Rapids: Baker, 1980), p. 367; William R. Read, Victor M. Monterroso, and Harmon A. Johnson, *Latin American Church Growth* (Grand Rapids: Eerdmans, 1969), p. 288.

## Local Autonomy

Few people are able to discuss the issues of either authority or local autonomy without finding the debate polarized. Participants on both sides of the debate over local autonomy can easily feel their rights have been violated by their opponents.

Donald L. Norbie, a Plymouth Brethren, insists,

> One searches the pages of the New Testament in vain to discover any traces of organizational unity between the local assemblies.... There was no organization into which each new assembly was received.... Each assembly was an independent, autonomous group which was not under the supervision of any other.... The union of early Christiandom was one on a spiritual level and not on an organizational plane....[8]

Others, however, insist that to focus on autonomy alone is to limit the heart of the issue. C. Peter Wagner, for one, has spoken for the identification of a congregation with the culture it serves in Christ's name: "A church planted on the mission field should so take on the characteristics of that culture that it is considered homegrown, or else it will never become a healthy, growing church."[9] Wagner maintains that a church can be self-governing, self-supporting, and self-propagating and still be a cultural misfit with no roots. The same view is shared by Hesselgrave.[10]

The heated debate relating to a mother church and satellite daughter churches centers on the practice of these satellites remaining tied to the mother church, either involuntarily or voluntarily. Norbie and others who agree with his view of autonomy maintain that where the Bible has spoken, we should stand against even culture if necessary. He insists that structural relationships are not an option to be modified from the biblical norm as each congregation may choose.

Actually, the concept of satellite churches has definite cultural advantages. An aggressive missionary mother church can extend its outreach into culturally diverse neighborhoods that have little or no strong Christian witness. This kind of church can exert leadership and provide an indigenous although not self-supporting ministry, because it has

8. Donald L. Norbie, *New Testament Church Organization* (Kansas City, Kans.: Walterick, 1977), pp. 26–27.

9. C. Peter Wagner, *Stop the World, I Want to Get On* (Glendale, Calif.: Regal, 1974), p. 91.

10. Hesselgrave, *Planting Churches Cross-Culturally*, pp. 366–67.

personnel, finances, and resources to commit to the point of greatest need.

## Optimum Size

Large churches with satellite groups combine the best of two growth strategies. They are unapologetically committed to the concept of the large church and tend to anticipate additional growth in the future. Most see their urban area as their parish and the multitudes as candidates for conversion and membership in their church. Although many of these churches are committed to building a large central church, most are just as committed to penetrating and reaching the city through the use of small groups coordinated fully, in most instances, by the parent congregation.

As more and more satellite locations are begun with limited space, limited trained leadership, and limited funds, new ways to provide additional space at the main site continue to be discovered. Some churches rotate Sundays that members from satellite locations can come to the main church. Almost all, however, provide multiple worship services each Sunday. Many of these churches also schedule multiple weeknight services that attract thousands.

Elmer L. Towns answered the question, "How large should a church be?" He wrote, "Small enough to allow for meaningful relationships between Christians so they can nurture one another, yet churches large enough (socially) to allow for individual differences."[11] He quotes Ralph Harris, editor-in-chief of Assemblies of God publications, and Dan Baumann, former pastor of Whittier Area Baptist Fellowship of Whittier, California, as saying that one minister can effectively pastor no more than three hundred members.

When asked by Win C. Arn, "What guidelines help us know how big a church should be before it starts planting another?" Donald A. McGavran responded,

> The matter of size is one which every church should face on its own. Many of my friends are inclined to say that when a church grows to more than four or five hundred members, its members cannot know other people, and at that point it should "hive" and start other congregations.[12]

11. Elmer L. Towns, "The Small, Personal Sunday School," *Christian Life*, April 1971, p. 48.
12. Donald A. McGavran with Win C. Arn, *How to Grow a Church* (Glendale, Calif.: Regal, 1973), p. 71.

Cho was once asked how many members he could successfully pastor without more than 10,000 cell groups. He answered,

> I don't think I could take care of more than 500. As it is now, I have to relate only to a relatively small number of leaders. These leaders have others under them who shepherd the cell leaders.... When a home cell group reaches a membership of more than fifteen families, it divides into two. After that, the two new cells invite new people until they both exceed fifteen families again, and then they divide into four.[13]

This congregation regularly receives 10,000 new members each month because it is able to reach and care for them through small groups.

## The Historical Model

Models for the church abound in literature about the church. A partial listing of these models can be found in Appendix B. The most usable models are those of Francis M. DuBose, F. W. Dillistone, Paul R. Orjala, James L. Sullivan, and White.

All three congregations that we shall study are base-satellite churches, to use one of DuBose's terms. They are organic-covenantal in Dillistone's categories. Each is the servant church of Dulles; the delegated church in Sullivan's terminology; and denominational (elder rule) by White's classification.

Ecclesiastically, however, the historic classifications—catholic, episcopal, presbyterial, and congregational—still stand. All three of the churches we shall consider are, in this writer's evaluation, either episcopal or presbyterial. Young Nak Presbyterian Church in Seoul is presbyterial; Yoido Full Gospel Church in Seoul is borderline episcopal/presbyterial; and Jotabeche Methodist Pentecostal Church in Santiago is also borderline episcopal/presbyterial.

Once a congregation of either presbyterial or episcopal governmental structure reaches a weekly attendance of about 5,000, the role of the ordained ministers tends to become increasingly episcopal. Although the congregation may occasionally be called into special business session to consider and voice opinions on highly significant issues, roles take on new meanings in these churches that have become minidenominations. The senior pastor (the title he uses makes little differ-

---

13. Cho with Hostetler, *Successful Home Cell Groups*, pp. 65–66.

ence) functions as a monarchal bishop to his staff or council of bishops in a figurative and functional sense.

At this point the issue becomes more intense as critics press for congregational autonomy as is described in Scripture.

## The Carnality of Competition

Perhaps the most common and blatant criticism against large churches concerns the motivation and even the integrity of those who lead them. Egotism is declared to be the primary motivation of the church and/ or its leaders.

Admittedly, egotism can be a problem. Any honest critic, however, is surely aware that this problem is neither isolated to, nor unique to, members and leaders of large groups. Egotism, as it is discussed here, usually takes the form of blind ambition. Symptoms of this malady often include compulsiveness, excessive pride, boastfulness, and an attitude that "the end justifies the means." However, for the Christian there is a remedy for this sin as well as for others.

Critics themselves seem insensitive to the high cost of egotism in the lives of those who have experienced it. They seldom rewrite the criticisms once those accused repent and make restitution for their sin.

Cho shares with his readers the high cost of egotism and untamed ambition early in his own ministry:

> In 1961 I decided to build the largest church in Korea. At that time I thought I was doing it for God, but today I realize that really I was doing it out of my own personal ambition. That proved to be a disaster. The Lord had to let me fail so that I would turn to Him in my need and allow Him to build His own church—in His own way.

> At that time we had a church of 600 members, a church that I had started three years earlier.[14]

## Buildings as Barriers

The large growing church, especially the congregation sponsoring satellite ministries, finds that it is helpful to know the structural and organizational alternatives before rapid growth occurs.

Knowing the functional limits of effectiveness for different structural

14. Ibid., p. 1.

models before those limits and limitations are tested is essential for meaningful and scriptural assimilation of members.

Ted W. Engstrom, president of World Vision International, explains this principle: "We must continue to face the truth that churches ... fail when they become prisoners of their buildings and lose their mobility, confining their activities within the walls of the sanctuary,without evangelism goals and a world missions strategy."[15]

Once existing facilities of a church become strained, a crisis point in continued growth has already occurred. Members and potential members often have already been lost before this point is reached. They have merely been replaced by a more aggressive variety of attender. The most aggressive, however, may also be mobile and temporary.

Often, the first stage of adapting to rapid growth is the creation of multiple services at the main facility. This, however, can compound the problem if the church finds itself getting larger while failing to care for those who attend. As participants have need of ministry and need to minister, small-group life is essential if growth is to continue.

House cell units outside the main church buildings can supplement available space in a valuable way. McGavran lists four ways home groups can assist unlimited yet person-centered growth: they eliminate the expense of buildings; they put minimum focus on the church's name or denomination; they reach new segments of society; and they bypass the obstacle of limited leadership.[16]

Four implications of structure listed by Snyder include, in abbreviated form: togetherness in one place at one time under the Holy Spirit's leadership, communication among members, informal structures that permit freedom of the Spirit, and church structure that provides Bible study in the context of community.[17]

Whatever else church buildings are good for, they are not essential either for numerical growth or spiritual depth. The early church possessed both these qualities and the church's greatest period of vitality and growth until recent times was during the first two centuries A.D. In other words,

15. Ted W. Engstrom, *What in the World Is God Doing? The New Face of Missions* (Waco: Word, 1978), p. 198.

16. Donald A. McGavran, *Understanding Church Growth* (Grand Rapids: Eerdmans, 1970), pp. 192–93.

17. Howard A. Snyder, *The Problem of Wine Skins: Church Structure in a Technological Age* (Downers Grove: Inter-Varsity, 1975), pp. 95–99.

the church grew fastest when it did not have the help—or hindrance— of church buildings.[18]

Russell E. Richey quotes John Wesley (1703–1791) concerning the goal of ecclesiastical order: "Is it not to bring souls from the power of Satan to God, and to build them up in His fear and love? Order, then, is so far valuable as it answers these ends; and if it answers them not, it is nothing worth."[19]

The aggressive church planting and evangelism carried out by growing large churches with structured satellite ministries demonstrate the soundness of Wesley's answer.

## Organizational Models

Leadership and organizational structure are the heart of this issue. Critics are polarized over the necessity of scripturally rooted models for leadership and organizational structure.

Hans Küng, a Roman Catholic, writes, "Today the task of theology should be to lay bare the original structures that have been covered over in the changes wrought by time. This ... is a necessary task."[20] Those in agreement with Küng include Augustus H. Strong and Alexander R. Hay.[21] They insist that Scripture is still the valid blueprint for all ages.

Among the opponents of the scriptural model or models as binding for today are Gene A. Getz, Arthur P. Stanley, and Edwin Hatch.[22]

Supporters of Scripture as the blueprint binding on churches built today are next required to outline what that blueprint's specifications require. Are the guidelines congregational, presbyterial, episcopal, or papal? The answer to this question, for the scripturalist, determines the validity of the large church with satellite groups.

18. Ibid., p. 69.

19. Russell E. Richey, "The Social Sources of Denominationalism: Methodism," in *Denominationalism*, ed. Russell E. Richey (Nashville: Abingdon, 1977), p. 173.

20. Hans Küng, *Structures of the Church*, trans. Salvator Attanasio (New York: Nelson, 1964), p. 394.

21. Augustus H. Strong, *Systematic Theology* (1907; Philadelphia: Judson, 1947), p. 896; Alexander R. Hay, *The New Testament Order for Church and Missionary* (Buenos Aires: SEMCA, 1947), p. 127.

22. Gene A. Getz, *Sharpening the Focus of the Church* (Chicago: Moody, 1974), pp. 82–83; Arthur P. Stanley, *The Epistles of St. Paul to the Corinthians* (London: John Murray, 1882), p. 280; Edwin Hatch, *The Organization of the Early Christian Churches*, 2d rev. ed. (1888; Austin: Quality Publications, 1976), pp. 216–22.

Critics supportive of extrabiblical authority (i.e., tradition and culture) are less apt to make an issue of the form as long as the functional performance reflects a reasonable image of New Testament expectations. Satellite groups administered by any of the various polities would probably, in varying degrees, meet the approval of these critics.

A brief consideration of administrative policy and practice is in order. This is the arena where laymen and ministry staff are most likely to experience conflict. Why must pastors and staff always be subdividing fellowship groups? The common phrase often used is, "Why do we split classes? Is it biblical and is it really necessary?" The first question has already been addressed. The answer to the second question depends on whom you ask.

Ask Towns and you will be told that need for the exercise is doubtful, for the key to growth is the charismatic leader rather than subdividing into small groups. During the 1970s movement was away from small classes in favor of the master-teacher method of teaching and the large Bible class. In the 1980s, however, the trend is back toward smaller classes.

> Many Americans do not want to become involved in small groups....
> The auditorium Bible class is the place where visitors can make a first contact with Bible study. As such, the ABC can become the handshake with the Sunday school. After visitors become involved with a master teacher in the auditorium setting, they can become involved in the smaller classes that meet their needs.[23]

This aversion to involvement in small groups may explain a general bias by American critics against the highly structured small satellite groups used in rapidly growing churches around the world.

Ron Jenson and Jim Stevens advocate the multiplication of subcongregations to encourage a biblical climate for numerical and nurturing growth.

> If a church is to grow, it must decentralize. It must expand its ministry to the subcongregations. The internal structure of the group gives leadership a chance to develop.... This commitment to and identity with a subcongregation provides an answer to the fear about a big church....
> It does not matter whether a church has two hundred or five thousand

---

23. Elmer L. Towns, John N. Vaughan, and David J. Seifert, *The Complete Book of Church Growth* (Wheaton: Tyndale House, 1981), p. 23.

members. Unless a church has only one hundred or fewer people, there is no chance of knowing everyone. In a large church, the secret is to quickly absorb people into subcongregations as a structure for meeting people.[24]

Jenson and Stevens admonish their readers that if the essentials of the "one-another" passages are to be experienced, small groups are essential.[25] Churches with satellite ministries specialize in small groups designed for both ministry and evangelism.

## Definitions of "Church" and "Minidenomination"

Traditional North American patterns of church growth are often challenged by radically different patterns and models found in other cultures of the world. Large parent congregations with networks of satellite chapels lead us to reexamine traditional definitions.

Jenson and Stevens make specific mention of this challenge by defining the authentic New Testament church as being ministry above mere celebration: "Christian leaders need to understand the contribution that a strong network of subcongregations makes to the whole body. For some churches this may involve a different definition of 'church.'"[26]

What actually constitutes a denomination? The answer given to this simple question will also determine the definition of the word *church*. Haste in defining one may lead to waste in defining the other. Sullivan notes that denominations have been known to have been begun by only a single man. Others are much more complex.[27]

The *Yearbook of American and Canadian Churches 1981* uses the three terms *churches, religious bodies,* and *denominations* interchangeably. A selective summary of religious bodies having few congregations and few members is presented in table 2.

With this information about denominations in hand, it is understandable how some writers consider the superchurches of the world to be

---

24. Ron Jenson and Jim Stevens, *Dynamics of Church Growth* (Grand Rapids: Baker, 1981), p. 142.

25. See Rom. 12:5, 10, 16; 13:8; 14:13, 19; 15:5, 7, 14; 16:16; 1 Cor. 11:33; 12:25; 16:20; 2 Cor. 13:12; Gal. 5:13; 6:2; Eph. 4:2, 32; 5:21; Col. 3:9, 13; 1 Thess. 3:12; 4:9, 18; Heb. 10:24; James 4:11; 5:9, 16; 1 Peter 1:22; 4:9; 5:5, 14; 1 John 1:7; 3:23; 4:7, 11.

26. Jenson and Stevens, *Dynamics of Church Growth*, p. 143.

27. James L. Sullivan, *Baptist Polity as I See It* (Nashville: Broadman, 1983), p. 70.

Table 2  **Small Denominations in the United States (1981)**

| Name of Religious Body | Number of Churches | Number of Members | Number of Pastors |
|---|---|---|---|
| *Christian Community and Brotherhood of Reformed Doukhobors* | 1 | 2,500 | 1 |
| *Church of Daniel's Band* | 4 | 200 | 4 |
| *Holy Orthodox Church in America, Eastern Catholic and Apostolic* | 4 | 260 | 4 |
| *The Bible Church of Christ, Inc.* | 5 | 2,300 | 5 |
| *Kodesh Church of Immanuel* | 5 | 326 | 5 |

Statistics are from the *Yearbook of American and Canadian Churches 1981,* ed. Constant H. Jacquet, Jr. (Nashville: Abingdon, 1981), pp. 225–32.

minidenominations. Each of the three congregations in this study exceeds the memberships of any of more than 120 denominations in the United States. Among those using the term *denomination* or *minidenomination* for the large congregations, many of which have a network of satellite ministries, are Lyle E. Schaller, Sullivan, Towns, and Charles L. Chaney.[28]

The foremost example of the satellite ministry in the United States is the Highland Park Baptist Church in Chattanooga, Tennessee. This 57,000-member congregation has approximately sixty satellite chapels. This is an Independent Baptist church and is most like other large satellite-ministry churches in the world.

Sullivan, in his discussion of the six basic denominational patterns, says,

An independent church is one which seeks to be a denomination within itself. It prefers one central location with massive meetings and highly visible activities. Such a church prefers that all smaller groups around dissolve and become a part of itself, even if they must be bused to one prearranged location far from their homes.[29]

28. Lyle E. Schaller, *The Multiple Staff and the Larger Church* (Nashville: Abingdon, 1980), p. 34; Sullivan, *Baptist Polity as I See It,* pp. 73–75; Elmer L. Towns, *America's Fastest Growing Churches: Why Ten Sunday Schools Are Growing Fast* (Nashville: Impact Books, 1972), pp. 190–91; Charles L. Chaney, *Church PLanting at the End of the Twentieth Century* (Wheaton: Tyndale House, 1982), pp. 166–67.

29. Sullivan, *Baptist Polity as I See It,* pp. 73–74.

## Parachurch Structures

Satellite groups directed by many of the largest churches are often classified by the parent congregation as mission or extension Sunday schools. The names given to these groups are as diverse as the countries where they are located.

Historically the Sunday school began as a movement that grew outside the local church and in some instances was even considered an agent for revolution. As a people's movement it was viewed with suspicion in England in the 1780s. Sunday-school societies were formed as what we now call parachurch groups. Many churches refused to allow Sunday schools to use their facilities.

Two centuries later, however, are we still justified in considering Sunday schools parachurch organizations? Snyder identifies Sunday school as a contemporary parachurch structure.[30] However, unless a mission Sunday school is conducted by parachurch organizations like the American Missionary Fellowship, established in 1824 as the American Sunday School Union, it is doubtful that Sunday schools can still be classified as parachurch. The primary issue is not parachurch structures, but rather autonomy.

Although establishing satellite groups may imply that a church has planted mission churches that are temporarily under the control of the parent church, this is not true in all cases. Some large congregations develop into superchurches and create mission or satellite groups designed from their inception to become independent, autonomous churches. Other large congregations, however, create missions or satellite groups (often called daughter churches) designed to remain a continual and integral ministry owned and operated by the mother church.

The key issue of the large church with satellite ministries has been well stated by Towns:

Can one group of people that have assembled in the name of Christ, control another group of Christian people? Or to ask the question differently, "Are Sunday school missions biblical, especially if they are never intended to be a church?" Then the churches of South America raise a question. Can one church own the property and control the ministry of another group of Christians; especially when the group may

30. Snyder, *The Problem of Wine Skins*, p. 166.

have 1000 members? Can one gathered church be divided into several smaller gathered assemblies?[31]

## Pastoral Care

Join a large church and you get lost in the crowd. Large churches are concerned only about numbers. Small churches are more personal and loving than large churches. True or false? Each of these statements can be either true or false, depending on how a church, large or small, views the spiritual gifts of its members and the importance of creating the kinds of groups that aid the assimilation and meaningful involvement of members into the life and mission of the church.[32]

Neil Braun is emphatic in his assertion that pastoral care is a major concern in effective and obedient world evangelism strategy.

> The need for pastors is indisputable. We do not question that every church needs pastoral care, or that it needs someone to administer the sacraments. The real question is: Who may properly be considered a "pastor," and who may properly administer the sacraments?

> The greatest problem in the world-wide missionary work of the church may well be the problem of how to provide pastoral care for the millions.[33]

Braun is a vocal advocate of equipping the rank-and-file members of Christ's churches to leave the church's unemployment lines and exercise their gifts for kingdom growth. He exegetes Mark 6:34 ("As he landed he saw a great throng, and he had compassion on them, because they were like sheep without a shepherd; and he began to teach them many things," RSV) to mean that pastors are not for church members exclusively. He insists that "pastors" are needed to detect and reach unsaved multitudes receptive to the gospel.

Among the large churches with satellite ministries in the United

31. Elmer L. Towns, *Getting a Church Started* (Lynchburg, Va.: by the author, Liberty Graduate School of Religion, 1982), p. 73.

32. For more information about this issue, see Lyle E. Schaller, *Assimilating New Members* (Nashville: Abingdon, 1978); Neil Braun, *Laity Mobilized: Reflections on Church Growth in Japan and Other Lands* (Grand Rapids: Eerdmans, 1971); Howard A. Snyder, *The Radical Wesley and Patterns for Church Renewal* (Downers Grove: Inter-Varsity, 1980); Cho with Hostetler, *Successful Home Cell Groups*; John W. Hurston and Karen L. Hurston, *Caught in the Web: The Home Cell Unit System at Full Gospel Central Church, Seoul, Korea* (Seoul: Church Growth International, 1977); Jenson and Stevens, *Dynamics of Church Growth* (chap. 12).

33. Braun, *Laity Mobilized,* pp. 39–40.

States, Asia, Africa, and South America, pastors and church members combine their resources and spiritual gifts to reach the masses with the gospel.

> Essentially what we need is an indefinitely reproducible pattern for church multiplying. We must recast our ideas so that it will become possible for any church, at any time, without outside assistance, to start a new church in its vicinity.
>
> We must reject the idea that every church must have (1) a paid pastor, (2) a pastor who has graduated from theological school, and (3) an expensive building. Let it be reiterated ... that they are not always necessary. These patterns are ... imported from Western Churches living and working under very different circumstances. They are neither found in, nor required by, the New Testament. They make church multiplication primarily dependent upon money, whereas the New Testament is almost silent on the matter of money for this purpose.[34]

The churches have the resources to fulfill the Great Commission. The personnel for assimilating the masses include ordained and lay volunteers, all exercising their respective spiritual gifts.

The structure through which these gifts are channeled are the groups of the church. Jenson and Stevens conclude, "The small group represents a more advanced stage of assimilation or absorption than does the subcongregation. The cell differs from the subcongregation in three important ways."[35]

The small groups (i.e., cells) are composed of three to ten people, designed to foster intimacy and accountability, and function best when the members are homogeneous.

The subcongregation is composed of between forty and a hundred people, designed to create a sense of belonging and identity, and usually a heterogeneous group including people of different ages, sexes, and backgrounds.

Eddie Gibbs adapts C. Peter Wagner's model for the three basic types of groups: cell, congregation, and celebration (see table 3). Balance between these three groups is essential if maximum assimilation is to be possible.

Large churches with satellite ministries, perhaps better than any other type of congregation, demonstrate how using gifted Christians

34. Ibid., p. 100.
35. Jenson and Stevens, *Dynamics of Church Growth*, pp. 146–47.

Table 3  **Types of Groups**

|             | Cell                              | Congregation             | Celebration                       |
|-------------|-----------------------------------|--------------------------|-----------------------------------|
| **Number of People** | 3–12                   | 13–175                   | more than 175                     |
| **Focus**   | people, personal, accountability  | task, social, activity   | event, community, celebration     |
| **Emphasis**| heart to heart                    | face to face             | neighbor to neighbor              |

This table relies on information from Eddie Gibbs, *I Believe in Church Growth* (Grand Rapids: Eerdmans, 1982), pp. 275–79.

and involving them in a balanced way through growth structures insures continued growth.

## Strategy for Urban Evangelism

Many of the world's largest churches are specialists at church planting. More than half of the twenty largest congregations in the world have an army of satellite groups.[36]

Statistics provided by McGavran and Arn graphically illustrate that nearly 30 percent of the population in the United States is actively Christian, 49 percent is nominally Christian, and 21 percent is non-Christian.[37] Of equal concern to missiologists at Fuller Theological Seminary is that between 40 and 50 percent of North America's population is isolated from receiving the gospel because of ethnic or cultural barriers.

McGavran postulates that the most effective tool for reaching the unreached is through planting new churches at the density of slightly less than one new church for each one hundred unchurched members of the population.[38]

With approximately 90,000,000 unchurched souls in the United States,[39] assuming that all could be reached and that none of these unchurched held membership in existing churches, 900,000 new churches are needed to reach them in this generation.

The issue of urban-evangelism strategy revolves around the challenge

36. John N. Vaughan, *The World's Twenty Largest Churches* (Grand Rapids: Baker, 1984).
37. Donald A. McGavran and Winfield C. Arn, *Ten Steps for Church Growth* (San Francisco: Harper and Row, 1977), p. 47.
38. McGavran with Arn, *How to Grow a Church*, pp. 135–36.
39. Chaney, *Church Planting*, p. 174.

to plant new church groups. Church leaders begin to be anxious when one mentions beginning new churches. There is some justification for their anxiety, because teams of existing members and resources are needed to begin these new units. Some churches naturally plant daughter churches, which is growth by extension, and often contribute to their own growth by expansion (i.e., enlarging the mother church).

Since most churches plateau by the time they reach 200 members, they also become static and passive. Unable to grow externally, they focus on internal nurture. Most of those baptized are their own children.

Any church that is experiencing rapid growth from expansion poses an automatic challenge and threat to neighboring churches whose growth is static. Usually members from the church with static growth will transfer to the larger growing church. Accusations of "sheep stealing" come naturally.

Growth through expansion is often traumatic for neighboring churches. The thought of growth through extension—beginning satellites in one or more locations—can generate rebellion from neighboring churches. This is tragic, for growth through extension is the only significant way the "pagan pool" can be reached.

The question of motive is always directed toward the large church that wants to plant groups in neighborhoods where other churches already exist. The burden of proof is always on the parent church, but even with pure evangelistic motives, transfer growth from neighboring churches will surely occur.

If the large church broadcasts on a local television station, the problem can be compounded. The large church has the greatest potential for growth merely because of its size and resources. However, other neighboring churches often become offended when members move to larger churches. A biblical basis for its own ministry and strategy is essential.

In an interview Wagner commented,

We have found the greatest resistance among churches growing at a rate of less than 100% per decade. These churches don't seem to have the surplus energy to think about new churches.

But often a church growing faster than 100% per decade is ready to start another congregation.[40]

40. James H. Montgomery, "Church Growth Flourishes in America," *Church Growth Bulletin*, November 1976, p. 88.

McGavran concluded, "We need multitudes of new churches which for maybe 5, 10, 15, 20 years are not bothered with a church building."[41] The biblical mandate allows no alternative to planting new churches when one considers that "according to our best calculations, each day welcomes a net increase of at least 78,000 Christians on this planet."[42]

## The Potential for Distorted Doctrine

In *The Community of the King,* Snyder discusses the risk of doctrinal impurity resulting from the multiplication of small groups and church communities. "Multiplication does increase the risk, for more life means more chance for aberrations. But there are safeguards. The most potent of these are the Spirit and the Word. . . ."[43]

A classic study of this very problem was conducted by Bishop Waskom Pickett, the missionary to India whose influence on McGavran has had considerable effect. This study is rooted in claims by some that converts coming to Christ in large group conversions (people movements) make poorer Christians and churchmen than those won as individuals.

Pickett interviewed 3,947 converts and measured their Bible knowledge and their effectiveness in their Christian life. Four areas of motivation (spiritual, secular, social, and natal) were used to evaluate the results. He concluded that postbaptismal followup, not motives for becoming a Christian, was the critical issue.

The bishop's studies indicated that, among the cases he reviewed, 90 percent of those not "spiritually" motivated at conversion were active in church, 90 percent of their homes were purged of idols, and 90 percent were financial contributors to the church.[44]

Churches involved in satellite ministries tend to have leaders who recognize the gifts of those they lead. Together there is a willingness to risk failure in the belief that "with men this is impossible, but with God all things are possible" (Matt. 19:26).

41. McGavran with Arn, *How to Grow a Church,* p. 136.
42. C. Peter Wagner, "Look at What God's Doing!" *Global Church Growth,* July/August 1983, pp. 296–97.
43. Howard A. Snyder, *The Community of the King* (Downers Grove: Inter-Varsity, 1977), pp. 130–31.
44. McGavran, *Understanding Church Growth,* pp. 150–52.

## The Strength of Churches

An interesting difference exists in the way churches in Brazil and many churches in North America think about beginning new satellite groups. North Americans tend to ask how many members the mother church should have in attendance before a new chapel can be begun. Churches in third-world countries frequently ask how many people they have to begin their next small house church. Brazil for Christ has considered these groups fully organized when they have gathered one hundred baptized members.[45]

In São Paulo, the Brazil for Christ Church functions as "a movement that plants churches." The mother church reports 14,000 members at the main location. Multitudes of small satellite groups have been planted. "The average organized church in the movement has ten small congregations that it has started and is responsible for. In other words, the Brazil for Christ Church is not only a mother, but in seventeen years is already a grandmother and a great-grandmother."[46]

These churches regularly endure the discomfort of beginning new satellite groups because their priority is a biblical fellowship centered in evangelistic outreach. Wagner compares the multiplication of these satellite groups in Latin America with cell reproduction in a healthy body.

> Biologically speaking, the cells in a healthy body are in a continuous process of division and multiplication. When the body of Christ is healthy, this will occur also. Effective evangelism not only seeks to win individuals and families and peoples to Christ, but to plant new churches as frequently as possible. There is nothing particularly Pentecostal about the mother-daughter church pattern. Any church can learn it and put it into practice.[47]

In conclusion, Snyder warns that a church should measure its achievements in terms of its birthing of spiritual children and grand-children rather than buildings and budgets.

45. C. Peter Wagner, *Look Out! The Pentecostals Are Coming* (Carol Stream, Ill.: Creation House, 1973), pp. 58–59.
46. Ibid., pp. 58–59.
47. Ibid., p. 63.

This is especially true of larger churches. Churches may only be getting fatter not healthier. . . . The mother church will not suffer, provided it is itself living and growing on biblical principles. If it is structured and depends heavily on a long roster of boards and committees, it will have difficulty producing new congregations. As I have already suggested, growth by division is an organic and charismatic process, not an institutional one.[48]

48. Snyder, *The Community of the King,* pp. 131–32.

# 2

# A Selective History of Large Churches, Past and Present

When most people think of large churches they envision gigantic cathedrals towering above the shops and homes of a European city. Actually, many of the cathedrals, for all their size, are far from full each Sunday. Their presence makes one wonder if they are the last of a former generation of other giants.

The size of cathedrals can only suggest to us today the multitudes that must have filled them, particularly for special occasions. Today the measurement and tabulation of the capacities of churches, the size of church memberships, and rates of membership gains and losses have become subjects of intense interest and research.

## The Early Churches

Christianity, both before and after the destruction of Jerusalem in A.D. 70, was often identified with Judaism. When one prospered the other often prospered and with persecution each experienced loss. While Jews considered Christians idolaters, the Romans viewed them as "atheists—

enemies of the gods.... Nothing was too bad to be believed of such people."[1]

Records indicate that nearly 200 synagogues were built along the shore of the Mediterranean Sea from the days of the temple in Jerusalem. The remains, partial or complete, of fewer than one hundred of them are still standing.[2] Mosaics and other Christian art indicate that some synagogues were adapted for Christian purposes.

The Talmud reports that before its destruction in A.D. 70, Jerusalem had 394 synagogues. Today's population in Jerusalem is four times larger than the estimated 100,000 of Jesus' day. Most of modern Israel's more than 6,000 synagogues still remain relatively small.[3] The synagogues early Christians assembled in are now scattered as rubble among the rocks of Judean hillsides.

One synagogue, the largest found to date, was unearthed in modern Turkey at Sardis, ancient capital of Lydia. Measuring 390 feet in length, it is larger than one of today's football fields.[4]

> The Talmud tells of a synagogue in Alexandria which was so large that the *hazzan* had to raise a scarf as a signal to the worshippers in the back who could not hear him, so they would know when to say "Amen." This story was often rejected as a gross exaggeration until the discovery in Sardis.[5]

The assembly area measured approximately 9,000 square feet, enough room for 1,000 worshipers to be seated on the floor. Most modern worshipers, however, fail to realize that until the seventeenth century, worshipers stood most of the time, knelt for short periods, and never sat.[6] This could significantly increase capacity. The Sardis synagogue also had a large gallery probably intended for use by the women.

> The Jewish presence in ancient Rome has always been known and well-attested.... Yet, strangely enough, although at least eleven different

1. Albert Henry Newman, *A Manual of Church History*, 2 vols. (Philadelphia: Judson, 1899), vol. 1, p. 149.

2. Hershel Shanks, *Judaism in Stone* (Washington, D.C.: Biblical Archaeology Society; New York: Harper and Row, 1979), pp. 11, 35.

3. Ibid., pp. 20–21.

4. Ibid., pp. 33, 171.

5. Ibid., p. 33.

6. Louis Bouyer, *Liturgy and Architecture* (Notre Dame, Ind.: University of Notre Dame Press, 1967), pp. 96–97.

synagogues ... are mentioned in Roman inscriptions, not a single ancient synagogue has been found in Rome itself.[7]

Well-meaning Christian leaders assume that church buildings did not exist during the first three centuries. However, Eusebius alone mentions eleven occasions of the destruction of already existing church buildings during the reign of seven Roman emperors.[8]

Our best records indicate that a variety of places were adapted by early Christians for their gatherings. These included homes, upper rooms, the temple, synagogues, hillsides, teaching halls, pagan temples, and particularly civic basilicas.[9] Prior to the reign of Constantine, "churches had long owned cemeteries, places of assembly, and all the paraphernalia of worship."[10]

J. G. Davies identifies nine early sources that attest to the existence of church buildings prior to 300.[11] (See Appendix C.)

J. W. Crowfoot mentions a quote from Eusebius's *Demonstratio Evangelica* (3:5, 108) where a comment is made "that up to the time of Hadrian's seige there was a very large church of Christ in Jerusalem which was constructed for Jews."[12]

Eusebius indicates the existence of "ancient" church buildings during the reign of Diocletian (284–305):

Who could describe those vast collections of men that flocked to the religion of Christ, and those multitudes crowding in from every city, and the illustrious concourse in the houses of worship? On whose account, not content with the ancient buildings, they erected spacious churches from the foundation in all the cities.[13]

He also writes, "There was an incessant joy, and there sprung up ... temples again rising from the soil to a lofty height, and receiving a splendor far exceeding those that had been formerly destroyed."[14]

7. Shanks, *Judaism in Stone*, p. 162.

8. Eusebius, *The Ecclesiastical History of Eusebius Pamphilus*, trans. Isaac Boyle (reprint; Grand Rapids: Baker, 1955), pp. 319, 320, 347, 348, 351, 377, 405, 427, 436.

9. Andre Bieler, *Architecture in Worship: The Christian Place of Worship* (Edinburgh: Oliver and Boyd, 1965), pp. 20–21.

10. Timothy D. Barnes, *Constantine and Eusebius* (Cambridge: Harvard University Press, 1981), pp. 49–50.

11. J. G. Davies, *The Origin and Development of Early Christian Church Architecture* (London: SCM, 1952), pp. 12–15.

12. J. W. Crowfoot, *Early Churches in Palestine* (London: Oxford University Press, 1941), p. 1.

13. Eusebius, *Ecclesiastical History*, p. 318.

14. Ibid., p. 405.

Then in 324 Emperor Constantine dedicated the former Saint Peter's Basilica in Rome. The basic rectangle of the sanctuary measured 330 feet by 200 feet. In the fifteenth century this building, with its four rows of twenty-five pillars each, was destroyed by Pope Nicholas V. The present Saint Peter's was then constructed (1506-1628).[15] With an estimated 66,000 square feet of worship space, the capacity in this sanctuary was probably more than 40,000 people. Constantine also built the Basilica of Saint John Lateran in Rome. The approximately 43,000 square feet of worship space may accommodate more than 20,000 people. The nave alone is 245 feet by 175 feet.[16]

Throughout the empire the new and largest basilicas served much the same functions as did the large cathedrals that would be erected throughout Europe, Great Britain, and South America beginning in the eleventh century. After defeating Licinius in 324, Constantine officially dedicated Constantinople as the capital of the Roman Empire in 330 and lived there almost continually. The construction projects of the empire shifted from Rome to Constantinople.

In *Early Churches of Palestine*, Crowfoot uses an interesting quote from Eusebius about chapels. Satellite chapels associated with today's superchurches are scattered throughout a city, but Eusebius notes that the church of the Holy Sepulchre at Mamre was large enough to have a block of buildings with rows of chapels.[17]

About 323 there were several Christian churches in Syrian Antioch, the third largest city in the Roman Empire. John Chrysostom, in his *Homilies on the Gospel of Matthew*, describes the largest as having 100,000 members. He even commented that if each member gave a loaf of bread and a love offering "no one would be poor."[18] Built on an island in full view of the local palace, the church was "Constantine's chief monument in Antioch and . . . was appropriate for the principal city of the eastern provinces."[19] This church was built by the emperor for celebration of major festivals and anniversaries. This era of building state churches was to become the model for European monarchs.

15. George Hedley, *Christian Worship: Some Meanings and Means* (New York: Macmillan, 1953), pp. 36-37.

16. R. F. Hoddinott, *Early Byzantine Churches in Macedonia and Southern Serbia* (London: Macmillan, 1963), p. 33. Estimates of space and capacity are those of John N. Vaughan.

17. Crowfoot, *Early Churches in Palestine*, pp. 9-10.

18. John Chrysostom, *The Homilies of St. John Chrysostom* (Oxford: John Henry Parker, 1851), p. 1124.

19. Glanville Downey, *Ancient Antioch* (Princeton: Princeton University Press, 1963), pp. 143-44.

During the first half of the sixth century Emperor Justinian began a vast building campaign. Among the thirty-three churches built and rebuilt by him in Constantinople and its suburbs, four are especially significant. Two of these are Hagia Ioannes (563), with almost 12,000 square feet of standing space for nearly 5,000 people, and Theotokos in Chalkoprateia (550), dedicated to the Virgin, with almost 12,000 square feet of standing space for nearly 5,000 people. The second largest, Hagia Eirene (Holy Peace), the first cathedral church of the city, had almost 14,000 square feet of space for more than 5,000 worshipers. Hagia Sophia (Holy Wisdom) was the grand cathedral. The main worship space was built with approximately 55,000 square feet of room for an estimated 20,000 worshipers. There were 110 doorkeepers assigned to this church.[20]

Hagia Sophia was intended by the emperor to be "the greatest church in the world" in a city of 600,000 people.[21]

> The great church dominated the whole of Constantinople. . . . It took five years to complete St. Sophia. The tradition was that ten thousand workmen were engaged on the building, under the direction of one hundred foremen. Before it was completed, Justinian fixed the staff of the church at sixty priests, one hundred deacons, forty deaconesses, ninety subdeacons, and one hundred readers and twenty-five singers to assist in the services. There were one hundred custodians and porters.[22]

## Changes in Patterns of Worship

Major changes in the New Testament pattern had begun to occur during the third and fourth centuries. During the next thousand years, from 400 to 1400,

> the altar once more became the seat of ancient sacrifices, with all the liturgical pomp they entailed. The holy priests no longer turned towards the congregation, as they still used to do in the apses of the more ancient basilicas. Now they turned their backs on the congregation and faced the sacrificial altar. . . . There was no longer a community of believers conducting their own worship. Instead there was a crowd who watched

20. Thomas F. Mathews, *The Early Churches of Constantinople: Architecture and Liturgy* (University Park: Pennsylvania State University Press, 1971), pp. 20–150.

21. Glanville Downey, *Constantinople in the Age of Justinian* (Norman, Okla.: University of Oklahoma Press, 1960), p. 21.

22. Ibid., p. 113.

the priests perform the service.... Thus from the fourteenth century onwards there appeared private chapels in the side aisle of the sanctuary.[23]

Andre Bieler insists that in evangelical worship, "a meeting-place is all that is necessary...."[24] He also refers to official action taken by the Church of Hesse in 1526:

We exhort all believers to participate in the prayers and public readings, regularly and with zeal, and similarly at the Lord's Supper. These acts of worship will no longer be carried out in the choir but in the middle of the church ... in concord and unity, for in Christ all are made priests.[25]

The era of great cathedral construction occurred in France, England, Germany, Italy, and Spain from the eleventh to the sixteenth century. In France, construction of the Cathedral of Notre Dame of Paris began in 1163. Canterbury Cathedral, the mother church of all England, was begun 1074 and completed in 1503. In Germany, Cologne Cathedral was dedicated in 1322 as the largest Gothic cathedral in northern Europe and is considered the mother of all German cathedrals. Spain's Cathedral of Seville, begun in 1402 and completed in 1519, is reported to be the largest Gothic building in the world. This cathedral has seven naves, thirty-seven chapels, and eighty altars. Fifty masses are celebrated in it each day. Rome's Saint Peter's Cathedral, originally built as a basilica in 324, had the first stone of the present building laid on April 18, 1506.[26]

Since Reformation years a definite shift had occurred in the structure of worship and the church. Renewed attention to the message of Scripture moved the major focus from the celebration-spectator role of the choir and mass to active member involvement; prophetic preaching replaced mere liturgical ceremony. In many sectors, the messages were primarily doctrinal and devotional and at times highly political.

The separated churches became state churches and defenders of the faith, but rarely missionary centers of evangelism.

23. Bieler, *Architecture in Worship*, pp. 43–46.
24. Ibid., p. 56.
25. Ibid., pp. 56–57.
26. Jay Jacobs, *Great Cathedrals* (New York: American Heritage, 1968), p. 330.

# Small Groups as a Means of Promoting Growth:
# A Brief Study of Two Approaches

### John Wesley and Methodism

Laws like the Conventicle Act of 1664 condemned as illegal any gathering of more than five people for religious purposes except as provided in the Book of Common Prayer. The Toleration Act of 1689 was not much better, for it still required that church meeting houses of dissenters be licensed by the government. This was the climate George Whitefield (1714–1770) and John Wesley (1703–1791) functioned in as ministers of the state church. A new chapter in the history of the large church was about to be written.

Denied freedom to preach in Anglican pulpits, Whitefield began field preaching. The May 9, 1739, issue of *The Gentleman's Magazine* reported this new movement of the unchurched masses:

> On Saturday the 18th Instant he preach'd at Hannum Mount to 5 or 6000 persons, amongst them many Colliers. In the evening he removed to the Common where ... were crowded ... a Multitude ... computed at 20,000 people.[27]

Howard A. Snyder illustrates how Wesley both understood and applied the simple genius of small-group dynamics to building the large church.

Wesley organized his followers into territories called circuits. They established a systematic plan for regularly visiting his followers by communities and cities. The circuits were composed of usually large groups known as societies. These were general gatherings whose only membership requirement was "a desire to flee from the wrath to come, to be saved from [one's] sins."[28] The society in Bristol had 1,100 members.

Dozens of societies were organized throughout Bristol and London. They were bound together under the name *United Societies*. All of the societies were responsible to Wesley personally.

Societies were subdivided into groups of twelve members each called

---

27. Quoted in Howard A. Snyder, *The Radical Wesley and Patterns for Church Renewal* (Downers Grove: Inter-Varsity, 1980), p. 32.

28. Sermon, "Of Former Times," *The Works of John Wesley*, ed. Thomas Jackson (London: John Mason, 1829–32), vol. 7, p. 250.

classes. "The class meeting was the cornerstone of the whole edifice. The classes were in effect house churches (not classes for instruction, as the term *class* might suggest), meeting in the various neighborhoods where the people lived."[29] These classes usually met weekly and could be led by either men or women.

Wesley further selected from among the classes those who professed assurance of salvation and organized them into bands. Each band was composed of five to ten members. Members of each society, class, and band who were in good standing were regularly issued tickets that provided admission to meetings. "It would appear that about twenty percent of the Methodist people met in bands, whereas all were class members."[30]

Finally, the elite among the bands were organized into even more intimate cell groups called select societies. These groups were for band members who "appeared to be making marked progress toward inward and outward holiness."[31]

The organizational structure designed by Wesley provided for rapid growth (see table 4).

According to E. Douglas Bebb, one in every thirty adult Englishmen was Methodist by 1800.[32]

How long can a movement as well-disciplined and organized as Wesley's be expected to experience dynamic growth? The transitory nature of both movements and large churches has already been mentioned. To answer this question researchers first must compare the

Table 4  **Growth of Wesley's Movement**

| Year | Decade | Number of Circuits | Number of Members |
|------|--------|--------------------|--------------------|
| 1768 | 1, 2, 3 | 40 | 27,341 |
| 1778 | 4 | 60 | 40,089 |
| 1788 | 5 | 99 | 66,375 |
| 1798 | 6 | 149 | 101,712 |

Data are adapted from information in Howard A. Snyder, *The Radical Wesley and Patterns for Church Renewal* (Downers Grove: Inter-Varsity, 1980), p. 54. Snyder's source is E. Douglas Bebb, *Wesley: A Man with a Concern* (London: Epworth, 1950), pp. 121–22.

29. Snyder, *The Radical Wesley*, p. 54.
30. Ibid., p. 60.
31. Ibid., p. 61.
32. E. Douglas Bebb, *Wesley: A Man with a Concern* (London: Epworth, 1950), p. 123.

duration of organizational life cycles of movements with and without satellite groups.

> The system of bands and classes instituted by Wesley continued for over a century. In England the bands disappeared about 1880 (the last band tickets were issued that year), while class meetings in both England and Ameria survived into the twentieth century, at least in some Methodist churches. . . .
>
> Well before 1900 the class system had lost its vitality, however, in most of Methodism. Where it survived, the classes often became legalistic or moralistic; the life had long since departed.[33]

Snyder continues by pointing out the parachurch nature of Wesley's traveling lay preachers (itinerants). He describes them as a "quasimonastic order" and points to this as an essential glue of the movement.[34]

Wesley's organizational structure assured him of an adequate supply of leaders for his cell groups. "Wesley put one in ten, perhaps one in five, to work in significant ministry and leadership."[35] The people he involved were common people, eager to serve. Snyder notes, "Community became the incubator and training camp for Christlike ministry."[36]

In addition to neighborhood cell groups, Wesley had a fully developed network of mission chapels. After transplanting his society model from Bristol to London, he planted chapels around his societies throughout the city. London became his parish (see table 5).

Table 5  **Wesley's London Chapels**

|  | Year Founded | Capacity |
|---|---|---|
| The Foundery Chapel | 1741 | 1,500 |
| The New Chapel | 1778 | 1,600 |
| West Street Chapel | 1743 | 1,800 |
| Wapping Chapel | 1741 | 1,000 |
| Spitalfields Chapel | 1750 | 1,800 |
| Deptford Chapel | 1757 | 600 |
| Poplar Chapel | 1772 | 250 |
| Snowfields Chapel | 1790 | — |

Statistics are from J. Henry Martin, *John Wesley's London Chapels* (London: Epworth, 1946), pp. 23–50.

33. Snyder, *The Radical Wesley*, p. 62.
34. Ibid., pp. 62–63.
35. Ibid., p. 63.
36. Ibid., p. 63.

J. Henry Martin describes the first chapel as a combination preaching hall, classroom, prayer room, book room, bookstore, and free medical dispensary. "It was much more than a preaching place; it was a community centre.... The Foundery became the first free dispensary in London. Alms houses followed the dispensary ... and the home for the aged poor...."[37]

To insure that each chapel began properly, Whitefield advised Wesley to purchase the property personally and have the title in his own name. Eventually he developed a system whereby the societies owned the property but he personally gained authority and responsibility for appointing pastors to the chapels.

### C. H. Spurgeon and the Metropolitan Tabernacle

After architects submitted sixty-two sets of building plans, London's Metropolitan Tabernacle was finally built and then opened to the public in March 1861.

Designed to seat 6,000, the Tabernacle had 25,225 square feet of floor space plus two galleries. Great care was given to the design of exits that allowed the building to be emptied in only five minutes. A congregation of more than 5,000 gathered weekly to hear the preaching of Spurgeon.[38]

Even the name of the church was intended to depict its mission and the zeal of its pastor for evangelism. The word *metropolitan* meant a citywide ministry; the term *tabernacle* was used because, as Spurgeon said, "We believe this building to be temporary, meant for the time in the wilderness without the visible King."[39]

After thirty years of ministry in the new building 14,460 had been baptized and received into membership. At one Communion Service one hundred were admitted, and one hundred and fifty at another time. In 1872 there were 571 new members added to the Church—the record year.[40]

"At his death in 1892, nearly nine hundred men had been trained in the ministry," according to W. Y. Fullerton.[41] The 1889 report for

37. J. Henry Martin, *John Wesley's London Chapels* (London: Epworth, 1946), pp. 24–26.

38. Eric W. Hayden, *A Centennial History of Spurgeon's Tabernacle* (Pasadena, Tex.: Pilgrim Publications, 1973), pp. 14–16.

39. Ibid., p. 14.

40. Ibid., p. 16.

41. W. Y. Fullerton, *Charles Haddon Spurgeon: A Biography* (1920; Chicago: Moody, 1966), p. 192.

the Pastor's College indicated that "students who had graduated had established over eighty churches in and about London and in all over two hundred churches in the world.... They had baptized over forty thousand. In America they had instituted fourteen different churches...."[42]

Spurgeon planted "five permanent mission stations" and operated a total of twenty-six satellite missions. He referred to them as "offshoots from the parent church."[43] Eric W. Hayden comments,

> Over twenty mission stations were founded within a few miles of the Metropolitan Tabernacle, with the aim of reaching the masses with the gospel of Jesus Christ. The workers of these "outposts" were largely Tabernacle members, although Spurgeon gave them a free hand in the running of the missions. Spurgeon himself was the "nerve centre," the one upon whom they could rely for advice, encouragement and support.[44]

A total of sixty-seven different ministries of the Tabernacle were announced, one at a time, during the great jubilee celebration on July 18, 1892. This list of societies of the church requires one and a half pages in *Spurgeon: The People's Preacher.*[45]

Listed among the societies are the Almshouses, the Pastor's College, the Evangelists' Association, the Ladies' Benevolent Society, the Loan Tract Society, the Orphanage Working Meeting, the Mission to Foreign Seamen, the Mission to Policemen, and the Coffee-House Mission.

## Large Churches in the United States (1800–1949)

Since 1800 several significant congregations in the United States have come and gone. Some have had satellite ministries; others have not.

Occasionally, large congregations are able to sustain continued growth for several decades before decline occurs. This ability to endure appears to be most common to churches with capable pastors who are able to lead one church for an extended time. Churches with effective small-group substructures appear most able to survive the latter min-

---

42. Russell H. Conwell, *Life of Charles Haddon Spurgeon, the World's Great Preacher* (Philadelphia: Edgewood, 1892), pp. 398–99.

43. Hayden, *A Centennial History of Spurgeon's Tabernacle*, p. 33.

44. Eric W. Hayden, *Searchlight on Spurgeon: Spurgeon "Speaks for Himself"* (Pasadena, Tex.: Pilgrim Publications, 1973), p. 120.

45. Reginald Henry Barnes, *Spurgeon: The People's Preacher* (London: Walter Scott, 1890), pp. 251–52.

istry of and transition from a long-term pastorate. Most, however, do not survive the transition once their leader either moves or dies.

The churches discussed in this chapter are representative of large churches from 1800 to 1949. Where possible the date indicated is the date the largest sanctuary was built.

>    1822—*African Methodist Church*, Charleston, South Carolina.
>        This congregation grew from 1,000 members in 1817 to 3,000 members by 1822 "in spite of the intolerant laws and the police regulations making it difficult for slaves and free persons of color to attend."[46] Morris Brown was pastor.
>    1832—*Chatham Street Chapel* (Second Free Presbyterian Church), New York City.
>        Led by Charles Finney, this congregation met in a renovated theater seating 2,500 to 3,000.[47]
>    1860—*Plymouth Church*, Brooklyn, New York.
>        Henry Ward Beecher regularly preached to 2,000 each Sunday in this church built for him.[48]
>    1869—*Calvary Church*, Chicago.
>        *Union Church*, Boston.
>        *First Presbyterian Church*, San Francisco.
>        These three churches, identified as three of the largest in America, each asked DeWitt Talmage in 1869 to become its pastor. He declined each invitation.[49]
>    1883—*First African Baptist Church*, Richmond, Virginia.
>        This church registered 2,675 members.[50]
>        *Sixth Mount Zion Baptist Church*, Richmond, Virginia.
>        Pastor John Jasper founded the church with nine members and led it to reach 1,068 members. Capacity of the building included 1,000 seats in the side galleries. He preached to as many as 2,000 at the church.[51]

46. Carter G. Woodson, *The History of the Black Church*, 3d ed. (Washington, D.C.: Associated Publishers, 1972), p. 67.

47. Ed Reese, *The Life and Ministry of Charles Finney* (Glenwood, Ill.: Fundamental Publishers, 1976), p. 11.

48. Ralph G. Turnbull, *A History of Preaching* (Grand Rapids: Baker, 1974), pp. 140–41.

49. Ed Reese, *The Life and Ministry of DeWitt Talmage* (Glenwood, Ill.: Fundamental Publishers, 1976), p. 7.

50. Woodson, *The History of the Black Church*, pp. 119, 140–43.

51. Richard Ellsworth Day, *Rhapsody in Black: The Life Story of John Jasper* (Valley Forge: Judson, 1953), pp. 84–85, 119.

1890—*Vermont Avenue Baptist Church*, Washington, D.C.
> This congregation was pastored by George W. Lee, who suc-
> ceeded J. H. Brooks, the founder of the church. "He soon
> attracted a large following and increased the membership of
> his church almost to 4,000."[52]

1890—*Bethany Presbyterian Church*, Philadelphia.
> Wilber Chapman as pastor was fortunate to have department-
> store magnate John Wanamaker as a member. On Easter
> Sunday, 1891, the "world's largest Protestant church" was
> dedicated. Regular attendance averaged 3,000 to 5,000. This
> church boasted the largest Sunday school in the world; the
> church and school building had a seating capacity of 4,820.[53]
> Chapman resigned in 1892 to conduct evangelistic crusades.
> He returned as pastor from 1895 until 1899. "With eight
> associates and assistants ... Sunday School membership
> reached a record high enrollment of 6,027 in 1898 to clearly
> make it the world's largest, and Bethany became the largest
> Presbyterian Church in North America. Church membership
> was 3,558 with ... over 16,000 signified professions of faith
> during his ministry there."[54]

1891—*First Baptist Church*, Dallas.
> The present church auditorium was built in 1890, prior to the
> coming of George W. Truett as pastor. He preached for almost
> half a century in this auditorium built to seat 2,800. The
> church had three satellite missions in 1897, eight in 1948, and
> seventeen in 1984.

> *Brooklyn Tabernacle*, Brooklyn, New York.
> DeWitt Talmage came to Central Presbyterian Church of
> Brooklyn when it had dwindled to only thirty-five members
> in March 1869. During his twenty-five years as pastor, he built
> the Tabernacle three times and saw it destroyed by fire three
> times. The first Tabernacle, dedicated in 1870 with seating for
> 3,500 people, was replaced in 1874 by a structure that would
> seat 5,000 people. Multitudes soon filled the new auditorium,
> since the opening of the new Brooklyn Bridge in 1883 meant

52. Woodson, *The History of the Black Church*, pp. 221–22.

53. Ed Reese, *The Life and Ministry of Wilbur Chapman* (Glenwood, Ill.: Fundamental Publishers, 1975), p. 6.

54. Ibid., p. 7.

that downtown New York City was a fifteen-minute drive away.[55]

Fire again destroyed the church buildings in 1889. The third and largest auditorium with seats for 6,000 people was dedicated on Easter Sunday, 1891. On many Sundays, 7,000 attended the church. "It was the biggest Protestant Church in the world. Talmage was now 59 years old."[56]

1894—*Chicago Avenue Church*, Chicago.

Built while D. L. Moody was pastor, this sanctuary seats 2,200 people. There are 1,200 seats on the main floor and 1,000 in the giant horseshoe balcony. Attendance averaged 2,700. At the funeral of evangelist Billy Sunday, a crowd of 4,400 was reported in the building.[57]

1907—*First Presbyterian Church*, Seattle.

When Mark A. Matthews became pastor of the church in 1902, the membership doubled in each of his first two years. A new auditorium seating 3,000 was built during his fifth year as pastor.[58] The church had an aggressive ministry with thirty satellite missions.[59]

1910—*Tabernacle Baptist Church*, Augusta, Georgia.

C. T. Walker served as pastor of this congregation for more than thirty-five years. "His church in Augusta was attended not only by thousands of his own race, but by hundreds of winter tourists.... Among these were President W. H. Taft, John D. Rockefeller.... He attracted larger crowds than any other Negro minister of his time."[60] Walker was vice president of the National Baptist Convention of the United States.

1920—*Olivet Baptist Church*, Chicago.

Under the direction of L. K. Williams, this congregation had 8,743 church members and 3,100 in Sunday school. "The

55. Reese, *The Life and Ministry of DeWitt Talmadge*, pp. 8–10.

56. Ibid., p. 7.

57. Roger Martin, *R. A. Torrey: Apostle of Certainty* (Murfreesboro, Tenn.: Sword of the Lord, 1976), p. 110.

58. William J. Larkin, "Matthews—Tall Pines of the Sierra," *Moody Monthly*, November 1974, pp. 83–86.

59. Randall Faulkner, "The Branch Church Ministry: An Innovation in Church Growth Strategy" (D. Min. diss., Trinity Evangelical Divinity School, 1984), chap. 2.

60. Woodson, *The History of the Black Church*, pp. 222–23.

church conducted forty-two departments and auxiliaries with 512 officers, among whom were twenty-four paid workers."[61]

1922—*Angeles Temple*, Los Angeles.

This center for the Four Square Gospel leader, Aimee Semple McPherson, was built for 5,400 attenders. In 1922 thirty-one weekly healing services were held in this auditorium.[62]

1924—*First Baptist Church*, Minneapolis.

William Jennings Bryan called William Bell Riley "the greatest Christian statesman in the American pulpit." Along with A. C. Dixon, pastor of Spurgeon's Metropolitan Tabernacle, he organized the meeting to draft the nine Fundamentals. Riley served as pastor of First Baptist Church from 1897 until 1942. After a Sunday-school campaign led by Louis Entzminger in 1920, the church grew and a new 2,634-seat auditorium was dedicated in 1925. The church was usually filled to capacity. Billy Graham conducted Riley's funeral in 1947.[63]

*Church of the Open Door*, Los Angeles.

R. A. Torrey, who served as pastor of Chicago Avenue Church (now Moody Memorial Church) from 1894 to 1905, organized and served as the first pastor of Church of the Open Door from 1915 to 1924.[64] In 1925 Riley was scheduled for a debate at the church filled with 4,000 eager witnesses. His opponent backed out at the last minute.[65]

1928—*First Baptist Church*, Fort Worth.

J. Frank Norris built the "world's largest Sunday school" at this location with a peak attendance of 12,000 at Sunday worship in 1928. Average attendance was 5,200.

While pastor of the Fort Worth church, Norris also built the Temple Baptist Church of Detroit in 1934; this church had 800 members. By 1943 this had increased to 8,597 members. This one man served churches with a combined membership

61. Ibid., p. 254.

62. International Church of the Four Square Gospel, Los Angeles, interview on 8 June 1983.

63. Ed Reese, *The Life and Ministry of William Riley* (Glenwood, Ill.: Fundamental Publishers, 1975), pp. 8–13.

64. Ed Reese, *The Life and Ministry of Reuben Torrey* (Glenwood, Ill.: Fundamental Publishers, 1975), p. 13.

65. Reese, *The Life and Ministry of William Riley*, p. 9.

of 25,000 people.[66] When Norris died in 1952, attendance declined in the Fort Worth church.

Temple Baptist Church probably could be considered the largest daughter (i.e., satellite mission) church birthed by any mother church in world history.

Among the twenty large churches listed, only three (along with Spurgeon's Metropolitan Tabernacle) are known to have had satellite-group ministries (see table 6).

## Large Churches in the United States (1949–1984)

In nearly three decades, 1949 to 1984, the trend toward large churches has continued in the United States.

In 1949, Akron Baptist Temple built a 2,500-seat auditorium. The church had come a long way since its beginning as a small Bible-study group of thirteen people. Prior to 1949 this church, under the leadership of Dallas Billington, reported 21,000 members. The Sunday-school attendance averaged 6,300 and the largest adult class had 2,500 in attendance. The record attendance for the church was 10,221 on Easter Sunday, 1943. During a thirty-three-year period, this church started more than 200 new churches.[67]

Also in 1949, a list of fifteen of the nation's twenty-five largest churches was published in a book by Louis Entzminger. *How to*

Table 6  **Churches with Satellite Groups**

|  | Number of Satellites |
|---|---|
| *First Presbyterian Church Seattle* | 30 |
| *Metropolitan Tabernacle London* | 26 |
| *First Baptist Church Dallas* | 8 |
| *First Baptist Church Fort Worth* | 1 |

66. C. Allyn Russell, *Voices of American Fundamentalism: Seven Biographical Studies* (Philadelphia: Westminster, 1976), pp. 30–31.

67. Elmer L. Towns, *The Ten Largest Sunday Schools, and What Makes Them Grow* (Grand Rapids: Baker, 1969), pp. 15–24.

*Organize and Administer a Great Sunday School* is the oldest compiled list of this kind known in recent times. Entzminger writes,

> Some years ago, after considerable research and investigation, I was able to make a list of the twenty-five largest Sunday Schools on the North American continent.
>
> I discovered that I had conducted enlargement campaigns, graded and reorganized, installed my system of records . . . plans and methods . . . in twenty-three of them.
>
> I do not claim credit for building these twenty-three largest Sunday Schools; but I claim that my work, plans and methods doubled and, in some instances, immediately tripled the attendance of these Sunday Schools. . . .[68]

Entzminger was serving as pastor of First Baptist Church in New Orleans until he was invited to become full-time Sunday-school superintendent for Norris, pastor of First Baptist Church of Fort Worth. He organized the Sunday school into groups, classes, and departments and led the church to report a thousand visits to members and prospects weekly. "By 1928 First Baptist Church had developed the world's largest Sunday school with 12,000 members and an average attendance of 5,200."[69] Norris died in 1952; Entzminger died in 1958.

Twenty years after Entzminger's book appeared, a similar book by Elmer L. Towns was published. *The Ten Largest Sunday Schools* also ranked the churches with the largest Sunday schools, but this list was released simultaneously with the research. By contrast, there was a time lag, although not an extended one, between the time Entzminger did his research and published his findings.

Also, whereas Entzminger gave only a partial listing of the twenty-five churches he studied, Towns gave a listing of only the ten largest churches, with full chapters on each. He also supplied an exhaustive chart of data for easy comparison of the churches. Fifty-one categories of information appeared in Towns's study.

From 1968 to 1978, *Christian Life* magazine, under Robert Walker as editor, enlisted Towns as Sunday-school editor to write an annual listing of the hundred largest Sunday schools in the country.

---

68. Louis Entzminger, *How to Organize and Administer a Great Sunday School* (Fort Worth: The Manney Company, 1949), p. iii.

69. Elmer L. Towns, John N. Vaughan, and David J. Seifert, *The Complete Book of Church Growth* (Wheaton: Tyndale House, 1981), pp. 92–93.

In 1981, the listing of the hundred largest Sunday schools was expanded in *The Complete Book of Church Growth*. In this book co-authored by Towns, John N. Vaughan, and David J. Seifert, churches were ranked by five categories: church membership, financial income, church (worship) attendance, Sunday-school enrollment, and average weekly attendance in Sunday school. (Refer to table 7 for a listing of the ten largest Sunday schools in these three surveys.)

Any time a list like this is made, there is the probability that one or more churches exist that should have been included. Personal investigation has revealed that at least three prominent Baptist congregations were omitted from the 1949 list. Among the churches known to be omitted in that list are First Baptist Church of Dallas, which was averaging 2,500 in Sunday-school attendance; First Baptist Church of Jacksonville, Florida, which was averaging 1,100 each week; and Bellevue Baptist Church of Memphis, Tennessee, which was averaging more than 1,000 each Sunday.

Table 7  **Comparison of Churches with the Ten Largest Sunday Schools**

| Rank | 1949 | Attendance | 1969 | Attendance | 1979 | Attendance |
|---|---|---|---|---|---|---|
| 1 | First Baptist Church Fort Worth, Texas | 5,200 | Akron Baptist Temple Akron, Ohio | 5,762 | First Baptist Church Hammond, Indiana | 15,101 |
| 2 | Temple Baptist Church Detroit, Michigan | 3,423 | Highland Park Baptist Church Chattanooga, Tennessee | 4,821 | Highland Park Baptist Church Chattanooga, Tennessee | 11,000 |
| 3 | Broadway Baptist Church Knoxville, Tennessee | 1,781 | First Baptist Church Dallas, Texas | 4,731 | Thomas Road Baptist Church Lynchburg, Virginia | 8,000 |
| 4 | Dauphin Way Baptist Church Mobile, Alabama | 1,745 | First Baptist Church Hammond, Indiana | 3,978 | Akron Baptist Temple Akron, Ohio | 6,700 |
| 5 | First Baptist Church Houston, Texas | 1,216 | Canton Baptist Temple Canton, Ohio | 3,581 | First Baptist Church Dallas, Texas | 6,600 |
| 6 | First Baptist Church Shreveport, Louisiana | 1,017 | Landmark Baptist Temple Cincinnati, Ohio | 3,540 | Westside Assembly of God Davenport, Iowa | 4,925 |
| 7 | First Baptist Church New Orleans, Louisiana | 902 | Temple Baptist Church Detroit, Michigan | 3,400 | Calvary Temple Springfield, Illinois | 4,908 |
| 8 | First Baptist Church Birmingham, Alabama | 853 | First Baptist Church Van Nuys, California | 2,847 | Corcord Baptist Church Brooklyn, New York | 4,800 |
| 9 | First Baptist Church Minneapolis, Minnesota | 801 | Thomas Road Baptist Church Lynchburg, Virginia | 2,640 | Canton Baptist Temple Canton, Ohio | 4,574 |
| 10 | Jarvis Street Baptist Church Toronto, Canada | 553 | Calvary Temple Denver, Colorado | 2,453 | Calvary Assembly Winter Park, Florida | 4,348 |

Statistics are from Louis Entzminger, *How to Organize and Administer a Great Sunday School* (Fort Worth: The Manney Company, 1949), p. iii; Elmer L. Towns, *The Ten Largest Sunday Schools and What Makes Them Grow* (Grand Rapids: Baker, 1969), pp. 154–63; and Elmer L. Towns, John N. Vaughn, and David J. Seifert, *The Complete Book of Church Growth* (Wheaton: Tyndale House, 1981), p. 356.
The list for 1949 required some revision. For example, Entzminger listed average Sunday-school attendance only for First Baptist Church of Fort Worth; in this chart statistics for the other churches have been added. (These statistics for 1949 were supplied by the churches.) Also, the figure for attendance for First Baptist Church, Fort Worth, is indicated in Entzminger's text as not being current. Finally, he identifies the church as having the largest Sunday school in the nation, but does not suggest that his original list of churches had changed.

Only First Baptist Church of Fort Worth had a satellite ministry in operation among the churches listed in 1949. The 1969 listing of the ten largest Sunday schools included three churches with satellite ministries. They are Akron Baptist Temple (Akron, Ohio), Highland Park Baptist Church (Chattanooga, Tennessee), and First Baptist Church (Dallas). The Akron church began 212 new Sunday schools.

Special mention should be made about evangelism methodology of churches in the 1969 survey. Nine of the ten churches had become involved in the bus-evangelism movement that was sweeping the country. Landmark Baptist Temple of Cincinnati led the group with seventy buses reaching 1,680 riders each Sunday. Close behind was First Baptist Church of Hammond, Indiana, with sixty-two buses and 1,500 weekly riders. Bus ministry served as both a diversion from and substitute for beginning satellite ministries, since buses brought the masses to the main church.

Different denominational groups are represented in each of the surveys. The 1969 list focuses mostly on Independent Baptist churches. Calvary Temple is the first charismatic church to be listed. In the 1979 list are included three Assemblies of God, one Southern Baptist congregation, five Independent Baptist churches, and the first black church to be included in a list (Concord Baptist Church). This large congregation is a daughter church planted by the nearby Abyssinian Baptist Church in Brooklyn. The mother congregation reported 18,000 members during the early 1960s when Adam Clayton Powell served as pastor.

Towns, commenting on the history of mission Sunday schools as an established method for beginning new churches, writes,

Using a mission Sunday School to plant a church is not a new technique. Actually, over 61,000 Sunday Schools were established by Sunday School missionaries employed by the American Sunday School Union between 1829 and 1879 in a campaign called the Mississippi Valley Enterprise. Many of these Sunday Schools evolved into Methodist churches.... If and when property is purchased, it is owned by the sponsoring church. The difference between a mission Sunday School and mothering a new church is that the mission Sunday School was not begun with the purpose of becoming an independent church.[70]

70. Elmer L. Towns, *Getting a Church Started* (Lynchburg, Va.: by the author, Liberty Graduate School of Religion, 1982), p. 67.

First Baptist Church of Dallas has used both the daughter-church and the Sunday-school approach with its seventeen missions. Almost all large churches with satellite chapels eventually have both types of missions, some by design and others by accident. Every mother church will eventually lose daughter churches who choose to leave the protective umbrella and become autonomous congregations.

Highland Park Baptist Church of Chattanooga, Tennessee, reports having sixty satellite ministries (mission Sunday schools). Resources for these branch churches are provided by the church's Tennessee Temple Schools.[71] The strategy of a large church establishing one or more schools to train satellite leaders has been popular since the time of Moody and Spurgeon.

At Florence Baptist Temple of Florence, South Carolina, Bill Monroe has also adopted the school approach. He has targeted nearly one hundred rural areas needing a ministry from his church. His goal is to begin one hundred mission Sunday schools in areas unable to support a church.[72]

Landmark Baptist Temple of Cincinnati created seven satellite churches out of previous bus routes. John Rawlings and his son Harold Rawlings serve as copastors of the mother church that averages 4,200 each week in Sunday school.[73] "The satellite churches are actually mission Sunday Schools except they include a preaching service where one of the staff members from the sponsoring church preaches."[74]

The Church on the Way of Van Nuys, California, has grown from a handful of members in 1971. Currently more than 4,000 people attend worship services each Sunday morning. One-fourth of this Four Square Gospel congregation, led by Jack Hayford, meet in homes every Sunday as members have rotated their attendance. The initial goal was 200 meetings in homes throughout the greater Los Angeles area.[75]

Peninsula Bible Church of Palo Alto, California, is known around the world through its pastor Ray C. Stedman and his most popular book, *Body Life*. The church is an independent congregation started almost four decades ago. The congregation is reported to have more than a

71. J. R. Faulkner, telephone interview at Highland Park Baptist Church, Chattanooga, Tennessee, July 1983.

72. Towns, *Getting a Church Started*, p. 67.

73. Harold Rawlings, telephone interview at Landmark Baptist Temple, Cincinnati, June 1983.

74. Towns, *Getting a Church Started*, p. 67.

75. Jack Hayford, *The Church on the Way* (Lincoln, Va.: Chosen, 1982), pp. 140–42.

hundred small satellite groups meeting in locations across the city. Most groups range in size from four to twenty members.[76]

Calvary Chapel of Santa Ana, California, has 15,000 members with a total of 35,000 persons who regard it as their primary spiritual resource center. Pastor Chuck Smith reports that 12,500 worshipers fill the 2,400-seat auditorium and auxiliary assembly areas each Sunday morning.

The church has rooms equipped with closed-circuit television for the overflow crowds during the four morning services. The 12,500 who attend are only adults above high school age. Other classes are provided for children in age-graded groups. Each Sunday, worship services are also conducted in Korean and Spanish at the main location.

Identified by many as the birthplace of the Jesus Movement, the church is only minutes west of Robert Schuller's Crystal Cathedral. As a church-planting congregation, Calvary Chapel has established 27 satellite chapels in Orange County and more than 210 nationwide.[77]

## Large Churches of the World

American church growth was a world unto itself until books by Donald A. McGavran and C. Peter Wagner began to appear. Large American churches were assumed by many to be the largest in the world. They were parasites at best and unbiblical at worst to the supporters of the small-group and underground-church movement of the 1960s.

The new mood in the decade of the 1970s was captured by Towns:

> God is beginning a new movement of super-aggressive churches across America. His Spirit has departed from most denominational churches. . . . This new movement of hyper-aggressive congregations spills over theological lines. They are found among the independent Baptists, Southern Baptists, Bible churches, Churches of God, Assemblies of God, Nazarenes, and many other groups. The super-aggressive church is the church of the future.[78]

76. "Six Churches: Thriving on Common Ground," *Christianity Today*, 21 May 1976, pp. 24–25.

77. Chuck Smith to John N. Vaughn, 2 August 1983, questionnaire on Calvary Chapel for *The World's Twenty Largest Churches* (Grand Rapids: Baker, 1984).

78. Elmer L. Towns, *Is the Day of the Denomination Dead?* (Nashville: Nelson, 1973), p. 155.

Any mention of "a new movement of super-aggressive churches" outside the United States is noticeably absent prior to 1970.

In 1965 American church leaders were captivated by the small-group movement. It was a time when not only large churches, but also churches in general, were viewed with disfavor. If there was an acceptable model for world missions, it probably would have been, in conservative circles, the legendary People's Church in Toronto, known for its enormous gifts to foreign missions.

That year, William R. Read's *New Patterns of Church Growth in Brazil* was published as part of a series about church growth.[79] Unnoticed by most American pastors, this book had two chapters that would, by the end of the coming decade, depict the dominant model for world church growth. The book was the story of explosive growth in Brazil, especially among the two indigenous Brazilian churches, *Congregacao Crista no Brasil* (Congregation of Christ of Brazil) and *Brasil para Cristo* (Brazil for Christ).

Both groups are composed of a multitude of satellite mission chapels perpetually maintaining membership in a very large mother church. Both churches are Pentecostal, large, minidenominational in structure, and Brazilian, meaning "foreign" and insignificant to most American church leaders. This was the era when "missionary go home" was commonly heard and many mainline denominations were withdrawing missionaries and terminating mission commitments in other countries.

Brazil for Christ's mother church alone has 14,000 members and only recently is reported to have released its satellite chapels as autonomous bodies. The chapel network extended beyond São Paulo to other cities and other states.

Brazil for Christ was reported to be constructing the world's largest church sanctuary, seating 25,000 people. Present capacity is probably closer to 10,000 or 12,000 at most. Read describes the facilities:

> The projected temple will enclose an area close to 12,000 square meters. It will contain a sanctuary that will seat 25,000, and there will be standing room under the roof for 15,000 more. The plans call for 46 different rooms, with a large library, a book store, a restaurant, a barber shop, and a tower 80 meters high that will hold 300 people on top.

79. William R. Read, *New Patterns of Church Growth in Brazil* (Grand Rapids: Eerdmans, 1965).

Elevators will whisk worshipers upstairs. Seven illuminated fountains and a small ornamental lake in front beautify the temple.[80]

Two years later, J. B. A. Kessler's *Study of the Older Protestant Missions and Churches in Peru and Chile* was published. In chapters 20 and 21 he describes the history of the Pentecostal movement's development in Chile, but especially the story of the Jotabeche Methodist Pentecostal Church in Santiago.[81] Today, that mother church and its forty satellite groups have more than 80,000 members.

Meanwhile, Towns's book, *The Ten Largest Sunday Schools,* was published in the United States in 1969. The popular acceptance of the book by American pastors once again created a climate highly receptive to developing large churches in this country. National interest became even more intense as the Institute for Church Growth at Fuller Theological Seminary began making the nation aware of church-growth movements outside the country.[82]

The Yoido Full Gospel Church of Seoul has nearly 500,000 members and is still growing at the rate of 10,000 new members each month. This phenomenal growth is aided by an organizational structure of 19,839 cell groups of about fifteen members each; 20,805 elders, deacons, and deaconesses; and 316 members of the pastoral staff. The congregation has three satellite ministries in Korea and has planted 118 churches outside Korea.[83]

Other large congregations in Korea and other countries are listed in table 8.

80. Ibid., p. 152.

81. J. B. A. Kessler, Jr., *A Study of the Older Protestant Missions and Churches in Peru and Chile* (Goes: Oosterban and le Cointre N.V., 1967), pp. 289-330.

82. A brief chronology of selected key publications gives a perspective of how intense the movement was becoming as Americans began to be informed about church growth in the third and fourth worlds: Donald A. McGavran, *Understanding Church Growth* (Grand Rapids: Eerdmans, 1970); C. Peter Wagner, *Look Out! The Pentecostals Are Coming* (Carol Stream, Ill.: Creation House, 1973); Towns, *Is the Day of the Denomination Dead?*; C. Peter Wagner, *Stop the World, I Want to Get On* (Glendale, Calif.: Regal, 1974); G. C. Oosthuizen, *Moving to the Waters: Fifty Years of Pentecostal Revival in Bethesda, 1925-1975* (Durban, South Africa: Bethesda Publications, 1975); John W. Hurston and Karen L. Hurston, *Caught in the Web: The Home Cell Unit System at Full Gospel Central Church, Seoul, Korea* (Seoul: Church Growth International, 1977); Paul Yonggi Cho, *The Fourth Dimension* (Plainfield, N.J.: Logos International, 1979); Nell L. Kennedy, *Dream Your Way to Success: The Story of Dr. Yonggi Cho and Korea* (Plainfield, N.J.: Logos International, 1980); Paul Yonggi Cho with Harold Hostetler, *Successful Home Cell Groups* (Plainfield, N.J.: Logos International, 1981); Paul Yonggi Cho with R. Whitney Manzano, *More Than Numbers* (Waco: Word, 1984).

83. Don Jones, telephone interview with Korean Baptist Mission in Seoul, 20 January 1984.

Table 8  **Satellite Groups among the World's Large Churches**

|  | Location | Number of Members (1982–83) | Number of Satellite Groups (1982–83) |
|---|---|---|---|
| *Young Nak Presbyterian Church* | Seoul | 60,000 | 25 |
| *Soong-Eui Methodist Church* | Seoul | 28,000 | 15 |
| *Sung Nak Baptist Church* | Seoul | 19,730 | 20 |
| *Choong Hyun Presbyterian Church* | Seoul | 14,000 | 50 |
| *Quang Lim Methodist Church* | Seoul | 13,500 | 1 |
| *Miracle Center* | Benin City, Nigeria | 10,000 | 28 |
| *Bible Baptist Church* | Cebu City, Philippines | 9,000 | 7 |
| *Evangelistic Center* | San Salvador, El Salvador | 5,600 | 200 |

The author gathered this information from the churches listed. Appendix A includes the text of the questionnaire used.

A significant contrast becomes increasingly obvious between American churches and those in other countries. Just as Sunday school and church buses are major vehicles for rapid evangelization of unchurched Americans, so the use of satellite groups is proving to be the most effective method of reaching the multitudes in other countries.

In Canada, the Beulah Alliance Church of Edmonton, Alberta, voted to begin its first satellite church more than thirty years ago. Their facilities were regularly being filled to capacity. A total of seven satellite churches were begun during the next two decades. The mother church has grown from 475 members to the present combined chapel attendance of 2,100 each Sunday.[84]

In the Soviet Union, the First Baptist Church of Moscow has a seating capacity of 1,600 and a combined attendance of 5,000 each Sunday in three services. Leningrad Baptist Church, with 3,000 members, fills its

84. Louis L. King, "A Rising Tide of Expectation," *Church Growth Bulletin*, September 1979, pp. 291–92.

sanctuary (which seats 1,200 people) in multiple services each week. Satellite groups are not possible.[85]

The Mo'en Church (formerly Moore Memorial Church) in Shanghai is the largest Christian congregation in that city of 12,000,000 people. "A staff of seven pastors and three Bible women, assisted by five retired clergy, carry on a team ministry by shepherding more than 6,000 Protestants in three Sunday services."[86]

In South Africa, Bethesdaland is a Pentecostal movement (Church of God, Cleveland, Tennessee) among the Indian community. It was begun in Durban in 1931 by the late J. F. Rowlands. Known since its inception as Natal's International Revival Center, it has grown to an estimated 36,000 members. Bethesda Temple, the church, has planted multitudes of satellite chapels. Until space became an overwhelming problem, chapels met in their communities during the week and then all assembled at the mother temple each Sunday. Several chapels in the satellite network, such as the large Shekinah Temple in Chatsworth with twelve chapels of its own, multiplied themselves rapidly. Due to development of new government housing in other nearby communities, the Indian population around the Bethesda Temple has moved away. Alex Thompson is now pastor and leader of the movement, which has been decentralized into autonomous churches.[87]

Douglas W. Slocumb, Coordinator of Communications for the Cleveland, Tennessee, Church of God World Missions department, recently wrote,

In Port-au-Prince, Haiti, we have a church which currently averages 3,000–5,000 in attendance per Sunday. Until recently, this church had several daughter churches throughout Port-au-Prince. The mother church and daughter churches together comprised a membership of 14,000. However, in the past few years, these daughter churches have been organized into independent churches.[88]

85. "Building 'Bridges' in Russia," *Worldwide Challenge*, April 1978, pp. 37–38.

86. P. Richard Bohr, "State Religion in China Today: Christianity's Future in a Marxist Setting," *Missiology*, July 1983, p. 329.

87. Correspondence with Alex Thompson, Full Gospel Church of God in South Africa, Durban, 15 March 1983.

88. Correspondence with Douglas W. Slocumb, Church of God World Missions, Cleveland Tennessee, 5 February 1982.

Just as Sunday school has been exported to churches in the third world, so evangelistic models from the world are being increasingly adopted by American churches. The satellite cell groups that encourage neighborhood nurture and evangelism have been adopted by large churches. For example, the 11,000-member First Baptist Church of Atlanta now has a full-time pastor assigned specifically to develop cell groups so the church can saturate Atlanta with the gospel of Jesus Christ and nurture its members.

In England several churches have adopted the satellite home-group method to achieve both extension and expansion growth. Eddie Gibbs has written about two of these churches:

> The church which best demonstrates this aspect is possibly St Michaels, York, with 69 people involved in leadership and with 508 people officially attached to groups, although by no means all attend. In my own parish of St Andrews Chorleywood, north of London, there are currently twenty-five home groups with an estimated 280 attending.[89]

Satellite groups, size, preference for independence of denominational affiliation, and even adaptability to diverse cultures do not make a church a New Testament church. These traits do, however, mark a method as being one that is able to thrive in a variety of soils that appear to have God's blessings. Chapter 3 will examine the biblical marks of a New Testament church and the implications for organizational structure.

89. Eddie Gibbs, *I Believe in Church Growth* (Grand Rapids: Eerdmans, 1982), p. 249.

# 3

## *Images of the Church*
### *A Search for Definitions*

... desire for numerical growth is biblical. The method of accomplishing this kind of growth will vary from church to church. Some churches will develop into "superchurches," whereas others will choose to develop "daughter" churches and to expand numerically by division.[1]

In this simple statement by Ron Jenson and Jim Stevens is the heart of a raging debate. Two kinds of large churches are described. The first, a "superchurch," is a single-base congregation that has no satellite "daughter" churches. This church's continued enlargement in membership and attendance is called expansion growth.

The second church makes a different decision and chooses to periodically encourage subgroups of the parent congregation to begin a new branch or satellite congregation. Normally, a parent congregation is called a mother church. The method of planting a satellite group at a location away from the parent church is called extension growth.

1. Ron Jenson and Jim Stevens, *Dynamics of Church Growth* (Grand Rapids: Baker, 1981), pp. 11–12.

"Extension" is a term that usually implies the mother church is willing to decrease in membership to insure a good nucleus to begin a daughter church.

Notice, however, that Jenson and Stevens used the verb *expand* rather than "extend" in describing the second church. Whether by accident or intent, they are saying that the network of daughter churches is designed to "expand" the mother church along with the satellite groups. This makes the satellite groups function as feeder groups for the mother church's own numerical expansion.

Heated debate centers around this issue. Many mother churches intend that their satellite groups remain perpetually under their authority. Can one church justifiably claim New Testament authority for exercising perpetual control over another congregation, even a daughter church? Can these satellite groups be scripturally defined as churches themselves? What is it exactly that makes a group a church? Is local autonomy a biblical concept or merely an assumption imposed upon the Bible by Christian interpreters in democratic societies?

Responses to these questions will be approached by examination of ten related issues, including the size of groups, a definition of the terms *church* and *satellite*, conversion as a prerequisite to membership, property, the relationship between movements and denominations, minidenominations, authority, biblical leadership, and autonomy.

## Identification of the Images

Earlier the distinction was made between cell, congregation, and celebration structures of the church.

> The instant a church pushes through a ceiling of 150, it consists of at least two or more subcongregations. These are groups with an affinity— geographical location, similar tasks within the church structure, or shared similarities of age, education, or professional interests.[2]

We have also seen that one congregation can be its own religious body or denomination. Gordon MacDonald has told us when a single-cell congregation functionally becomes two churches under one roof. Is there a minimum number of people that can still constitute a church?

In table 9, the groups are listed with the total number of confirmed

2. Gordon MacDonald, "Ten Conditions for Church Growth," *Leadership*, Winter 1983, p. 46.

Table 9 **A Comparison of Average Congregation Size among Church Groups**

| | Number of Confirmed Members | Number of Churches | Average Size of Congregation |
|---|---|---|---|
| *African Methodist Episcopal (A.M.E.)* | 1,970,000 | 3,050 | 646 |
| *American Baptist Churches in the U.S.A.* | 1,271,688 | 5,897 | 216 |
| *Assemblies of God* | 958,418 | 9,562 | 100 |
| *Church of God Cleveland, Tennessee* | 411,385 | 5,018 | 82 |
| *The Episcopal Church* | 1,962,062 | 7,022 | 279 |
| *The Lutheran Church, Missouri Synod* | 1,965,422 | 5,689 | 346 |
| *Presbyterian Church in the U.S.* | 852,711 | 4,067 | 210 |
| *Southern Baptist Convention* | 13,372,757 | 35,552 | 376 |
| *United Methodist Church* | 9,653,711 | 38,576 | 250 |

Statistics are from the *Yearbook of American and Canadian Churches 1981,* ed. Constant H. Jacquet, Jr. (Nashville: Abingdon, 1981), pp. 225–31.

members divided by the total number of churches to determine the average congregation's membership.

Can a home prayer meeting justifiably be called a house church? Edward D. O'Connor, associate professor of theology at the University of Notre Dame, points to the pastoral direction of the apostles (Acts 2:42) and later their appointment of elders (Acts 14:23; 20:28).

> A church does not arise wherever two or three Christians meet together in Jesus' name, but only when they are called together by one who is a bearer of the apostolic authority ... (Hebrews 13:7)[.] Holding prayer meetings in private homes is a good way to foster Christian life; but it does not take the place of the church.[3]

John F. Walvoord, president of Dallas Theological Seminary, warns,

3. Edward D. O'Connor, "Evangelical Leaders Assess Home Churches," *Christian Life,* 1 January 1982, p. 32.

The so-called "house church" movement is built upon the fallacy that if we go back to worshipping in a house, as the early church did, we will have the same spiritual power as they had.... It is of course, not true that all the early churches met in houses. Undoubtedly in many cases, they had to rent a hall or secure a larger meeting place.... Even our Lord, in observing the passover feast in which the Lord's Supper was instituted, rented a place. And most of His preaching was outdoors to large crowds, which could not enter a house.[4]

Others, however, like Karl Barth and John Wesley, view the issue in a totally different manner. Wesley, quoted by Howard A. Snyder, insists, "Even two or three united in Christ's name, or a Christian family, may ... be called a church."[5]

Large churches with satellite groups frequently face the issue of house churches. The house as a center for evangelism is very common outside the United States.

In our discussion we have affirmed the key role of the large congregation for both expansion and extension growth. We have defined the debate over mother churches that often maintain perpetual authority over their satellite chapels. As we now turn to an examination of a biblical definition of "congregation," evaluations are being made to determine if a satellite group can be classified biblically as a congregation.

Jenson and Stevens express their concern that many churches have failed to define and relate to their own networks of subcongregations.

For some churches this may involve a different definition of "church." Most people define "church" as celebration. "Did you go to church today?" means "Did you go to the Sunday morning worship service?" The New Testament does not endorse such a definition, because the New Testament emphasizes ministry to and with one another. Celebration meets the need for corporate worship, but it cannot provide involvement in each other's lives.[6]

Someone has said that the heart of the church must be as big as the world but as small as one soul. The pages of the New Testament

4. John F. Walvoord, "Evangelical Leaders Assess Home Churches," *Christian Life*, 1 January 1982, p. 32.

5. Quoted in Howard A. Snyder, *The Radical Wesley and Patterns of Church Renewal* (Downers Grove: Inter-Varsity, 1980), p. 73.

6. Jenson and Stevens, *Dynamics of Church Growth*, p. 113.

repeatedly call us back to the vital role of member involvement in the lives and ministry of others in the body of Christ (e.g., Acts 2:42–45; 4:32–35; 5:12–16; 8:4–8). Even Solomon recognized the principle (Eccles. 4:9–12).

Charles R. Swindoll, pastor of First Evangelical Free Church of Fullerton, California, vividly depicts the intensity of the tension that he experienced as the pastor of a large growing congregation.

> I distinctly remember the first time I read that our congregation was referred to as a "super church." I felt uneasy about the label.... But I couldn't get around it, our numerical size gave us the label.... Can't size and depth coexist.... How can a large church that attracts so many people from such varied backgrounds harness the energy and move people from mere spectators to participants.... The secret is a firm commitment to assimilation.... I began to speak on the value of becoming involved in a small-group ministry....[7]

Swindoll defines assimilation as "becoming absorbed in the function of the Body of Christ as an active participant, relating to, sharing with, and caring for others in the Body."[8] He therefore encourages involvement in small-group ministries such as adult fellowship groups, choirs, evangelistic teams, prayer groups, weekly home Bible classes, men's and women's groups, and special groups that deal with local ministry needs.

Some people-helper groups begun by Swindoll's church include a Single Parents' Fellowship, a Breadwinners in Transition group for the unemployed, and Children of Dependent Adults for those with the responsibility of caring for aged or disabled relatives.

As early as 150, Justin Martyr recorded a description of the New Testament church:

> We are always together with one another. And for all the things with which we are supplied we bless the Maker of all through his Son Jesus Christ and through his Holy Spirit. And on the day called Sunday there is a gathering of all who live in a city or a rural district.[9]

7. Charles R. Swindoll, *Dropping Your Guard: The Value of Open Relationships* (Waco: Word, 1983), pp. 17, 25.

8. Ibid., p. 25.

9. Justin Martyr, *Apology* 1, 67:1–3, 7, quoted in Everett Ferguson, *Early Christians Speak* (Austin: Sweet, 1971), p. 67.

This extrabiblical report depicts a single centrally gathered church ministering to a total urban population. It also indicates that all the believers in that city gathered each Sunday for worship. Throughout the world, large growing churches tend to see themselves as the major worship, evangelistic, and teaching centers of their cities. These large churches function like a temple among synagogues, although in New Testament times there existed differing functions between the two institutions.

Whereas Justin Martyr describes the gathering at a central location each Sunday, Eusebius (c. 320) mentions Christians in Emperor Valerian's palace:

> For never was there any of the emperors before him so favourably and benevolently disposed toward them, not even those who were openly said to be Christians, so plainly received them, with such excessive civility and friendship in the commencement of his reign. All his house was likewise filled with pious persons, and was, indeed, a congregation . . . of the Lord.[10]

When Christian leaders gathered in August 1948 at Amsterdam to found the World Council of Churches, Earl D. Radmacher notes, the moderator began immediately to call for a definition of the church. He reports the moderator as having said, "The first fact to face is that there is no agreed Christian interpretation of the doctrine of the Church."[11]

Radmacher, devoting intense energies to review every major definition and interpretation of the church, discusses five indications of what the church is not and five marks of the New Testament churches.

First, Radmacher insists that the church of the New Testament is never a physical structure, a state or national church, a denomination, the kingdom of God or the kingdom of heaven, or designated as Israel.[12]

Second, he lists five marks of the New Testament church as described in Scripture. Scripture demands a regenerate membership that includes only the saved and all of the saved, an autonomous membership in relation to other churches and civil government, an ordered and pur-

10. Eusebius, *The Ecclesiastical History of Eusebius Pamphilus*, trans. Isaac Boyle (reprint; Grand Rapids: Baker, 1955), p. 278.
11. Earl D. Radmacher, *What the Church Is All About: A Biblical and Historical Study* (Chicago: Moody, 1972), p. 11.
12. Ibid., pp. 161–86.

poseful membership as evidenced by gifts and government, a unified membership void of ecumenical union while evidencing local unity, and a growing membership in both nurture and numbers.[13]

The whole issue of what constitutes a church extends far beyond the need to define the nature of satellite groups and their relationship to a mother church.

A minor crisis developed over this same issue with the University Baptist Church of Manila in 1983. The 2,500-member congregation operates twenty mission points, has fifteen seminary-trained staff, and baptized 500 in 1982. Their goal is to have forty missions. The church is located in the center of Manila's university belt, a small section of the city where 300,000 students attend about one hundred universities. Many of the deacons are students. The issue of student deacons is where the problem began with some of the members.

John Rutland, staff member of the Baptist state paper in Texas, reported,

> Some people have accused the church "of not really being a church," saying all age groups are needed. But with 65,000 students across the street and no other Baptist church in the area, Cabalang [the pastor], 42, is happy with the make-up of his congregation. . . .
>
> The church membership is divided into small groups, because "when a church becomes big it has a tendency to become impersonal. We don't do this." . . . The groups are training cells that have produced 200 trained counselors who work out of the student center.[14]

A catalogue could be filled with definitions of "church." Roman Catholic definitions, like that of Robert Cardinal Bellarmine, emphasize sacraments and the apostolic succession and appointment of bishops and priests.[15] John Calvin focuses on the "Word of God purely preached and heard, and the sacraments administered according to Christ's institution."[16] Martin Luther's definition of church accents the sacraments and the presence of the gospel. Luther deemphasizes place as essential to any definition of the church.

13. Ibid., pp. 338–65.

14. John Rutland, "Riotous Times Spawned University Church, Manila," *Baptist Standard*, 27 July 1983, p. 9.

15. L. Harold DeWolf, *A Theology of the Living Church* (New York: Harper and Row, 1953), p. 323.

16. John Calvin, *Institutes of the Christian Religion*, ed. John T. McNeill, trans. Ford Lewis Battles, 2 vols. (Philadelphia: Westminster, 1960) vol. 1, p. 9.

The essence, life and nature of the church is not a bodily assembly, but an assembly of hearts in one faith.... Thus, though they be a thousand miles apart in body, yet they are called an assembly in spirit because each one preaches, believes, hopes, loves and lives like the other.

The external marks, whereby one can perceive where this Church is on earth, are baptism, the sacraments, and the Gospel; and not Rome, or this place, or that.[17]

Free-church leaders who live under the shadow of state churches in other countries stress that two essential marks of a church are, first, voluntary acceptance of the gospel for salvation rather than automatic infant baptism into the state church at birth and, second, the autonomy of the local church.[18]

The church as a "convened assembly" called together by God himself and the separation of his saints from the world are recurring themes for Adolf Deissmann.[19]

French ecclesiologist Alfred Kuen expressed repeated conviction that the church must be composed of believers and not the unconverted masses. He is speaking against the European state-church baptism of unconverted infants.[20]

A converted membership, nurture, service, and evangelism plus the "planting of new congregations throughout the world" are essential to David J. Hesselgrave's definition of the church.[21]

James L. Sullivan, a noted Southern Baptist, spotlights the importance of the work the church is called to rather than what the people have been called from. Mission is primary with Sullivan; this is revealed in his definition of church as "a body of baptized believers, bound together voluntarily by the common bond of love for Jesus Christ working together under God's Holy Spirit to do his work on earth."[22]

Church of Christ ecclesiologist Monroe E. Hawley discusses the

17. Martin Luther, *Works of Martin Luther*, 6 vols. (Philadelphia: Holman, n.d.), vol. 1, p. 361.

18. Gunnar Westin, *The Free Church Through the Ages*, trans. Virgil A. Olson (Nashville: Broadman, 1958), pp. 1–2.

19. Adolf Deissmann, *Light from the Ancient East* (New York: Harper and Brothers, n.d.), p. 112.

20. Alfred Kuen, *I Will Build My Church*, trans. Ruby Lindblad (Chicago: Moody, 1971), p. 253.

21. David J. Hesselgrave, *Planting Churches Cross-Culturally: A Guide for Home and Foreign Missions* (Grand Rapids: Baker, 1980), p. 20.

22. James L. Sullivan, *Baptist Polity as I See It* (Nashville: Broadman, 1983), p. 19.

meaning of the word *ekklesia*: "Its basic import is that of a gathering of citizens called out of their homes. It is used in this sense in Acts 19:39 where we read, 'But if you seek anything further, it shall be settled in the regular assembly.'"[23] He magnifies the larger assembly rather than a house-church ministry.

The missionary background of Conservative Baptist leader George Patterson shows in his definition: "These are repentant, baptized believers who celebrate the Lord's Supper, love one another, show compassion to their neighbors, pray, give, and evangelize."[24]

Elmer L. Towns, an Independent Baptist, accents "discipline of the Word of God, organized for evangelism ... and reflecting the spiritual gifts." His full definition says, "A church is an assembly of baptized believers, in whom Christ dwells, under the discipline of the Word of God, organized for evangelism, education, fellowship and worship; administering the ordinances and reflecting the spiritual gifts."[25]

Among the several definitions given to this point, only Gunnar Westin writing on the stance of the Free churches, Sullivan, and Towns place evangelism and mission higher than other functions of the church (e.g., worship) in their definitions.

Finally, Christian Lalive d'Epinay provides the first definition of church that includes a reference to both mother churches and satellite chapels.

> The *congregation* is the local church, with its principal place of worship and its chapels, its pastor and council. The term congregation is specifically valuable in the case of Pentecostalism and Methodism, which are organized on the 'congregational' model, in which all the local churches are quite autonomous and rank equally with one another. As a synonym, we shall often use the term community.[26]

D'Epinay is one of the few writers to deal specifically with two essential areas in his definition. Special note should be made of his references to "its principal place of worship and its chapels" and "its

---

23. Monroe E. Hawley, *Redigging the Wells* (Austin: Quality Publications, 1976), pp. 84–85.

24. George Patterson, "The Spontaneous Multiplication of Churches," in *Perspectives on the World Christian Movement: A Reader*, ed. Ralph D. Winter and Steven C. Hawthorne (Pasadena, Calif.: William Carey Library, 1981), p. 603.

25. Elmer L. Towns, *Getting a Church Started* (Lynchburg, Va.: by the author, Liberty Graduate School of Religion, 1982), p. 18.

26. Christian Lalive d'Epinay, *Haven of the Masses: A Study of the Pentecostal Movement in Chile* (London: Lutterworth, 1969), p. xxxiii.

pastor and council." Notice too that he merges both the "principal place . . . and its chapels" under the common category *the local church.* His assertion is that the

Principal Place + Chapels = The Local Church

In the United States the satellite chapels tend to be viewed as mission outposts, annex Sunday schools, and preaching halls. Those reached through these centers are included in the membership of the mother church.

Mother churches often view the satellites as branch Sunday schools merely located away from the main site of the church. They all seem to encourage some of the units to become autonomous churches. Many churches would never consider releasing a satellite chapel any more than the average American church would consider having an adult Sunday-school department, inside the church, meeting independently of the main church.

Towns diagrams the differing roles of a local church and a mission Sunday school (see table 10).

First Baptist Church of Dallas, with more than 25,000 members, illustrates the relationship of chapels to the mother church. W. A. Criswell, pastor of the church for forty years, has led the congregation to develop a network of seventeen chapels and about ten preaching points.

Chapels operated by the Dallas church are of two types. The first type of chapel is intended to become an independently organized church.

Table 10  **Local Church and Mission Sunday School Contrasted**

| **Local Church** | **Mission Sunday School** |
| --- | --- |
| Self-Supporting:<br>Controls income and purchasing. | Depends on sponsoring church.<br>Property owned by sponsoring church.<br>Offerings go to central treasurer. |
| Self-Propagating:<br>Can reproduce itself. | Ministry is led by Christians from sponsoring church.<br>Mission people help in ministry. |
| Self-Governing:<br>Able to direct itself and is not controlled by outside influence. | Decisions for ministry and organization made by sponsoring church. |

From Elmer L. Towns, *Getting a Church Started* (Lynchburg, Va.: by the author, Liberty Graduate School of Religion, 1982), p. 68. Used by permission.

We found them, organize them, mother them, care for them until they are able to carry on their own ministries, then we commend them to the grace of our Lord and let them go on their own. Some of the finest and largest churches in the city of Dallas have been started by us in this program.[27]

The second kind of chapel is usually located among the poorer areas of the city and often is intended to reach minority groups. Criswell indicates that the church once had a chapel that began to grow rapidly and functioned well until the mother church decided the chapel was ready to be organized into a separate church.

We did so only to invite disaster. In a short time the church was torn asunder by warring sections and factions. They lacked the ability to govern themselves. We were forced to take it back, give it Christian leadership, and it has been a chapel ever since, getting along splendidly as long as we run it.[28]

Criswell also indicates that all of the mother congregation's benevolent ministry is accomplished through the chapels.

The maturity and skills for self-government are just as critical for the parent church as they are for the chapel. As surely as some chapels may not be considered mature enough to function effectively without the mother church, so also there are established churches that are not ready to plant and parent another church.

Sherman Williams describes the kind of church that ought to become involved in planned parenthood of new chapels. His presupposition is that a church should grow only so large and then focus on reproducing itself through new satellite chapels. The method he recommends is to begin with about fifty members from the mother church and assistance from a staff member loaned from the mother church. He insists that unless a church is itself winning people to Christ, it has no business attempting to plant a church.

As a pastor of the Redwood Chapel Community Church of Castro Valley, California (near San Francisco), Williams has planted chapels and understands both sides of the issue.

27. W. A. Criswell, *Criswell's Guidebook for Pastors* (Nashville: Broadman, 1980), p. 185.
28. Ibid., pp. 185–86.

A growing church can consider itself prepared to reproduce by starting other churches when it is effectively winning people to Christ, when it provides the ranges of services that meet the needs of its members and when the body is maturing because every cell member is being ministered to and is ministering to others.[29]

Williams indicates that when his church plans to parent a new church, it enters into a firm agreement with the nucleus group selected to begin the church that it too will plant more satellite ministries. Great efforts are made to insure a "like mother, like daughter" attitude in church planting. A mother church mobilizes her members and resources for evangelism as the new church is led to the point where it can stand alone.

Five tasks or functions of each church, mother and daughter, that are needed to fulfill its purpose as a New Testament church include worship, education or indoctrination, caring and community building, mission or outreach, and self-government that leads to goals, roles, and priorities. "The particular way a given congregation carries out these five core tasks will vary according to the congregation's size, resources, location, and other factors."[30]

Patterson has researched strategy for beginning satellite groups among Baptists in Honduras and offers several building blocks for this type of evangelism. He defines eight basic terms:

*Mother Church*—a congregation which mobilizes men in another locality to raise up and pastor their own church.

*Daughter Church*—a congregation raised up within an extension chain by a mother church.

*Extension Center*—a place other than a resident seminary or institution where classes are held (usually by one or more churches) to train and mobilize Christian workers for immediate service.

*Subcenter*—an extension center operated by a *student* of another center.

*Extension chain*—the process of church reproduction in which a mother church with an extension center starts one or more daughter churches which in turn become extension centers and start more churches.

*Dead-End Link*—a local church which fails to become a mother church.

*Lay Pastor*—a volunteer, part-time worker trained and licensed by his

29. Sherman Williams, "Mothering Churches," *United Evangelical Action*, Summer 1977, p. 24.

30. David R. Ray, *Small Churches Are the Right Size* (New York: Pilgrim, 1982), p. viii.

own congregation to baptize, lead the Lord's Supper, and serve as a pastor.

*Student Worker*—a Christian who receives training on the job. He puts his extension studies into *immediate practice.*[31]

Patterson then offers five guidelines for establishing an extension chain for perpetual evangelism and growth:

1. Urge the newborn church to mobilize its members for continued reproduction.
2. Promote the extension student to be a student-teacher.
3. Do not let building programs stop the chain—don't let anything stop it.
4. Evaluate constantly the progress of each student and teacher in the chain.
5. To continue the chain indefinitely, seek out student-teachers who will simply repeat these same steps.[32]

A constant danger to be aware of is gathering the masses and admitting them into the membership of the church although they have not experienced genuine conversion to Jesus Christ. Observers and leaders of churches have sounded this alarm on numerous occasions. Kuen, J. Gresham Machen, Theo Lehmann, Luther, and others consider this a grave problem.[33]

The Bible warns us to avoid the critical error of measuring ourselves by ourselves and ourselves by others (2 Cor. 10:12).

Emperor Constantine is reported to have baptized 12,000 men, women, and children in 324. There was only one slight problem with his mass coversions. This was not a typical people movement. He is said to have offered every "convert" twenty pieces of gold and a white baptismal robe.[34]

31. George Patterson, "Multiplying Churches Through Extension Chains," *Church Growth Bulletin,* July 1974, pp. 427–28.

32. Ibid., pp. 432–33.

33. See Kuen, *I Will Build My Church,* p. 208; J. Gresham Machen, *Christianity and Liberalism* (Grand Rapids: Eerdmans, 1923), pp. 159–160; Theo Lehmann, "The Gathering of the Congregation," *The Gospel and the Ambiguity of the Church,* ed. Vilmos Vajta (Philadelphia: Fortress, 1974), p. 129.

34. Albert Henry Newman, *A Manual of Church History,* 2 vols. (Philadelphia: Judson, 1899), vol. 1, p. 307.

Churches planning to begin satellite churches need to be aware that once buildings are erected for them, dynamics that previously did not exist begin to operate. Wesley discovered that with his first chapel; he had to decide who would own the property. He planned for the chapel to own the land and property, even though he paid for it himself with cash, but his friend George Whitefield advised that it was a grave mistake for the chapel to own the property until the chapel matured under his leadership.

Another decision Wesley had to make was what he would name the chapel and the others that followed. He had to call them preaching houses because to call them meeting houses would have obligated the chapels to pay taxes and would also have identified his chapels with other groups considered radicals. Also, although he considered himself a loyal member of the Church of England, his church properties eventually played a major role in the break of Methodism from the state church and in the ordination of pastors. One final concern that became a major chapter in his life was how to insure that chapels would remain true to the faith. If members of a chapel wandered from the covenant of the faithful, would they retain the property purchased and built by the parent church? These are but a few of the issues one leader of a parent church had to face.[35]

Snyder, in a critique of church buildings, says they attest to five facts about the church today: immobility, inflexibility, lack of fellowship, pride, and class divisions. "The fault here of course lies much deeper than mere architecture. But the building is a witness. It is a signpost telling the world of the church's class consciousness and exclusiveness."[36]

Donald A. McGavran, writing about the benefits of house churches for early Christians, notes that "at one stroke they overcame four obstacles to growth": building costs; a fixation on the synagogue, liberation from which allowed movement into Gentile communities; introversion that prevents Christian homes from being evangelistic centers; and limited leadership as all able men were pressed into kingdom service.[37]

The initial period of planting a new church is critical to the formation

35. E. Benson Perkins, *Methodist Preaching Houses and the Law* (London: Epworth, 1952), pp. 13–14.

36. Howard A. Snyder, *The Problem of Wine Skins: Church Structure in a Technological Age* (Downers Grove: Inter-Varsity, 1975), pp. 69–73.

37. Donald A. McGavran, *Understanding Church Growth* (Grand Rapids: Eerdmans, 1970), pp. 192–93.

of that congregation's concept and definition of its evangelistic strategy. According to Kuen,

> There is absolutely no need for vast edifices in order to begin the work; the apostolic phrase 'the church in ... house' (Ro 16:5; 1 Co 16:19; Col 4:15) is still perfectly suitable for all churches at their inception. The place for the reunion grows as the community grows, and increasingly material needs are met by the growing membership.[38]

Snyder and others intimate that an excessive preoccupation with place, property, and problems is a factor in losing momentum for growth.

The pastor of one large mother church with more than 10,000 members refers to his church as "a movement that plants churches."[39] There is a thin line between being a movement and a denomination. It is the same kind of thin line between the superchurch being a mini-denomination or a denomination. H. Richard Niebuhr quotes Ernst Troeltsch, historian of the social ethics of the churches:

> The really creative, church-forming, religious movements are the work of the lower strata.... All great community building revelations have come forth again and again out of such circles and the significance and power for further development in such religious movments have ... made this impetus absolute and divine.[40]

A movement is a spirit of commitment to a venture and cause that transcends denominational domains. During the early stages of a movement the focus is on a particular cause and is able to attract followers from a variety of groups.

Movements eventually lose their initial energy and become more passive. This can be brought about by a change in significant issues, a change in leadership, or other transitional events. Russell E. Richey speaks of a denomination as being the displaced memory of a movement that lost its spirit.[41] Sociologists describe a denomination as being like a fossil. First-generation ancestors of the denomination are often

38. Kuen, *I Will Build My Church*, p. 271.

39. C. Peter Wagner, *Look Out! The Pentecostals Are Coming* (Carol Stream, Ill.: Creation House, 1973), p. 59.

40. H. Richard Niebuhr, *The Social Sources of Denominationalism* (1924; New York: Meridian, 1957), p. 29.

41. Russell E. Richey, "The Social Sources of Denominationalism: Methodism," in *Denominationalism*, ed. Russell E. Richey (Nashville: Abingdon, 1977), p. 170.

labeled sects. A sect usually is homogeneous in make-up, is oriented toward a single issue, and places priority on action and results rather than contemplation and consultation. Sects are leader-oriented, whereas the denomination is usually oriented toward group decision.

Although Luther and Wesley were more Puritan than Separatist, Luther considered himself a good Catholic and Wesley took pains to verify his authenticity as a loyal Anglican. Neither man had any intention of separating from his parent denomination. Neither realized that he was a leader of a movement on the way to becoming a denomination.

The superchurches discussed in the previous chapter are denominational churches, almost without exception. A unique feature is that almost all are led by the founding pastor. If it is not headed by the founding pastor, the church is usually led by the pastor who guided the church to experience unusual growth. He is functionally a founder, although historically he is not. Church members even treat him as if he is the patriarch of the group. Although these churches are denominational and are affiliated with national and international bodies, each appears more like a sect.

Any definition of a single congregation with more than 10,000 members automatically raises issues that do not apply to a church with 100 members. Also, any church with 10,000 members and satellite chapels has already asked itself questions a 100- or even 1,000-member church has never asked. For example, questions of organizational strategy, communication, and the biblical guidelines for leadership can vary widely.

Are superchurches with thousands of members denominations? The word *denomination* literally means "to have a name." Wesley is credited in church circles with having first made the word popular.[42]

Church of Christ leader Hawley defines the term:

A denomination is a group of professed Christians with an existence that is not identical to the entire body of Christ. At best it is but part of the church having separated itself by its actions from other disciples of Christ. At worst it may be argued, it is not a denomination at all since it is not even Christian.[43]

42. Winthrop S. Hudson, "Denominationalism as a Basis for Ecumenicity: A Seventeenth-Century Conception," *Denominationalism*, ed. Russell E. Richey (Nashville: Abingdon, 1977), pp. 21–22.

43. Hawley, *Redigging the Wells*, p. 22.

Independent Baptist Towns says,

A denomination is a group of churches with similar doctrinal beliefs, who have similar traditions and backgrounds, who share the same goals in ministry, who desire fellowship to encourage one another, and have organically bound themselves together to establish corporately what they feel cannot be wrought separately.[44]

D'Epinay writes,

The term denomination signifies a particular organized religious movement which has been given a name and has a controlling body. In addition, in sociology this concept has a distinct content and signifies a definite type of religious organization.[45]

Elsewhere, Hawley lists five characteristics of a denomination. He indicates that all are not necessary to indicate that a group qualifies. Only one is needed by his definition. The five marks are a legislative or executive organization foreign to God's Word, an authoritative creed, a basic doctrine which contradicts the Word of God, a distinctive name which "denominates" it and separates it from others, and a sectarian attitude.[46]

By the definitions already listed, the larger churches of the world would all qualify as denominations, except by Town's definition. His qualification *group of churches* would exclude large, independent churches, with or without satellite groups, as long as the satellites are justifiably regarded as extension Sunday schools and not churches.

All of the large churches tend to be very conscious of authority. Cyprian declared that where the bishop is, there is the church. Conversely, if there is no bishop, there is no church. Most pastors of the superchurches both appoint and delegate to those who lead under them. The majority function as monarchal bishops and several (those in independent churches) as metropolitan bishops.

The priesthood of believers is one of the dominant doctrines practiced in these large churches. The branches are places to discover gifted lay

44. Elmer L. Towns, *Is the Day of the Denomination Dead?* (Nashville: Nelson, 1973), pp. 49, 118.

45. D'Epinay, *Haven of the Masses,* p. xxxiii.

46. Hawley, *Redigging the Wells,* pp. 22–24.

leaders. From these branches pastors frequently recruit members to fill major leadership roles within the church.

Kuen lists men and women used powerfully by God, but who had no formal theological training: the twelve disciples, Francis of Assisi, Calvin, George Fox, William Booth, William Carey, Hudson Taylor, C. T. Studds, Adoniram Judson, C. H. Spurgeon, D. Martyn Lloyd-Jones, Watchman Nee, John Bunyan, and Blaise Pascal. Fox was a shepherd, Booth was a businessman, Carey was a cobbler, Lloyd-Jones was trained as a physician, Bunyan was a tinsmith, and Pascal was a mathematician and philosopher.[47]

## Isolating the Issue: Biblical Autonomy?

Is there a biblical basis for satellite groups? The issue here is autonomy within the local church. The issue is also one of leadership structure of the church.

> No subject in Church history has been more hotly discussed than the organization of the primitive Christian Church.... There seems to have been in the Church several forms of organization, and to some extent the various contentions of conflicting creeds and politics have been therein justified.[48]

Joseph Cullen Ayer continues by pointing out that although there were geographical pockets of churches governed by an episcopal form of government, this form "seems not to have been universally diffused at that time."[49]

In *The Historic Church*, J. C. V. Durell poses the case for a staggered development of the threefold orders of bishops, presbyters, and deacons. He indicates that by the early second century, Ignatius had substantiated that from Syria to Troas the threefold formula had been adopted. Macedonia had not yet adopted the structure; Polycarp's letter to the Philippians is void of any reference to bishops.[50]

As the bishop of London, J. W. C. Ward, wrote,

47. Kuen, *I Will Build My Church*, pp. 264–65.
48. Joseph Cullen Ayer, *A Source Book for Ancient Church History from the Apostolic Age to the Close of the Conciliar Period* (1913; New York: AMS, 1970), pp. 35–36.
49. Ibid., pp. 35–36.
50. J. C. V. Durell, *The Historic Church: An Essay on the Conception of the Christian Church and Its Ministry in the Sub-Apostolic Age* (1906; New York: Kraus, 1969), p. 13.

Throughout the first three centuries no very clear line of demarcation was drawn between the ordinary life of the clergy and that of the laity. The clergy for the most part earned their livelihood at secular trades ... until in the fourth century ... withdrawal began to be represented as a matter of obligation. In the early days the line between clergy and laity was drawn below the three offices of bishop, priest and deacon. ... [51]

The second and third centuries marked an isolation of the laity from their biblical role as priests. Everett Ferguson identifies Clement as the first to use the term *laity* in Christian literature outside its biblical context of 1 Peter 2:5, 9. "The organizational history of the second and third centuries ... is not the story of the emergence of the priesthood but the emergence of a distinct laity not exercising a priestly ministry."[52]

The Pentecostal pastor in Chile today is often contrasted with the Protestant pastor. A product of academic training, the Protestant pastor is viewed as a cleric, whereas the Pentecostal pastor, no matter what authority he holds, is "simply a church member who has reached the top of the ladder, while the whole community continues to bear the evangelistic ministry."[53]

Autonomy as a biblical issue, at its simplest level, is a matter of who has the authority to exclude a member. Passages touching on this question include Ephesians 5:11 and 2 Thessalonians 3:6. What we want to know first is, what does the Bible say about the autonomy of the local church?

Of the 117 uses of the term *church* in the New Testament, B. H. Carroll says, "All but five (Acts 7:38; 19:32, 39, 42; Hebrews 2:12) refer to Christ's *ecclesia*. ... These 113 uses of the word ... refer either to the *particular assembly* of Jesus Christ on earth or to his *general assembly* of glory."[54]

W. L. Hayden lists the only three tribunals authorized in Scripture: the elders of a local church (Acts 14:23; 20:28; 1 Tim. 5:17; Heb. 13:7, 17); wise men able to judge between brothers (1 Cor. 6:5); and the elders of sister churches (Acts 15:1-6).[55]

Hayden is supported by Flavil R. Yeakley, Jr. (Church of Christ).

51. J. W. C. Ward, *A History of the Early Church to A. D. 500* (London: Methuen, 1937), pp. 119-20.

52. Everett Ferguson, *Early Christians Speak* (Austin: Sweet, 1971), p. 172.

53. D'Epinay, *Haven of the Masses*, p. 77.

54.* B. H. Carroll, "Ecclesia, the Church," in *Studies in the New Testament Church*, ed. Louis Entzminger (Fort Worth: The Manney Company, n.d.), p. 27.

55. W. L. Hayden, *Church Polity* (Chicago: S. J. Clarke, 1894), p. 143.

Yeakley identifies Acts 15:22 and 6:1–6 as texts often used by those who propose local autonomy. He merely identifies them as "good examples of the kind of communication that is needed for an open style of leadership."[56] He adds that the American preference for democratic majority rule is imposed upon Scripture and a New Testament church that is a monarchy, a kingdom, under the rule of King Jesus.

The process outlined by Yeakley has Jesus delegating limited authority to local churches which then elect elders. At that point, "the decision-making authority of the congregation as a whole is transferred to the eldership. . . . The system which many denominations use to make decisions by the majority vote of the congregation is not Scriptural."[57]

In response to Yeakley, it seems only fair to let the scriptural record speak for itself. On numerous occasions the church is seen making its own decisions under the Holy Spirit's leadership (Acts 6:1–6; 11:22–26; 15:22; 2 Cor. 8:16–20). One of the strongest claims in Scripture for the authority residing within the local congregation is found in Matthew 18:15–18. Jesus instructs his disciples, who were apostles, that if a troublemaker refuses correction from the apostles, the next level of appeal is to "tell it to the church." If that effort fails, Jesus says, "let him be unto thee as an heathen man and a publican" (v. 17). Jesus then indicates that the action of the church is final and is binding in both heaven and earth (v. 18).

Later, Clement of Rome in his *Epistle to Corinthians* (44, 54) affirms the role of the whole congregation.[58] Acts 6:3, 5 indicates that the congregation "chose" the men and the apostles "appointed" them.

Louis Entzminger summarizes his own convictions about the matter:

This power of the church cannot be transferred, church action is final. That there is no tribunal higher than a church is evident from Matthew 13:15–17. . . . But can there be no appeal to an association or presbytery or conference or convention? No, there is no appeal.[59]

56. Flavil R. Yeakley, Jr., *Church Leadership and Organization* (Arvada, Colo.: Christian Communications, 1980), pp. 35–37.

57. Ibid., pp. 35–37.

58. Clement of Rome, "Epistle to Corinthians," in J. B. Lightfoot, *The Apostolic Fathers* (1891; Grand Rapids: Baker, 1956), p. 36.

59. Louis Entzminger, ed., *Studies in the New Testament Church* (Fort Worth: The Manney Company, n.d.), p. 70.

The model prescribed in Scripture is that of a plurality of elders (bishops, Acts 20:17-19, 28) and deacons. Elders were appointed in "every church" (Acts 14:23; 20:17; Phil. 1:1; 1 Tim. 5:17). Plurality of elders is indicated (Acts 20:28; Phil. 1:1; 1 Tim. 3, 5:17; 1 Peter 5:1-4).

Apostolic authority is specifically referred to on three occasions.[60] Two references are made by Paul in 2 Corinthians (10:8; 13:10) and one in 1 Thessalonians (2:6). J. Ridley Stroop, in his commentary on these verses, concludes,

> From the New Testament teaching it is clear that the apostles had no teaching of their own. Neither is their inclination to depart from God's teaching, which had been delivered unto them. They taught, they encouraged, they exhorted people to do the will of God.[61]

Stroop indicates that their work was always cooperative in nature, never dictatorial (Acts 6:1-6; 8; 15:2; Gal. 1:17-18; 2:1-10). Again, Clement of Rome (c. 150) could write about his own ministry as an elder, "If by reason of me there be faction and strife and division, I retire, I depart, whither ye will, and I do which is ordered by the people: only let the flock of Christ be at peace with its duly appointed presbyters."[62]

These passages in no way are meant to minimize texts that stress the scriptural duty of the churches to follow their pastors as bishops (1 Cor. 14:37; 1 Thess. 5:12-13; 1 Tim. 5:17-18; Heb. 13:7, 17, 24).

Next among the issues related to autonomy is that of episcopacy, or rule of a major bishop over brother bishops and their congregations. One of the stronger claims opposing the episcopacy is that of G. H. Lang. Following his references to 2 Corinthians 1:1, 8:1, 1 Corinthians 1:2, Galatians 1:2, and Acts 9:31, he promptly opposes "any scheme or form of interlocking of assemblies."[63]

German theologian Hans Küng quotes Pope Leo XIII, who says of other bishops, " . . . one must not consider them as vicars of the Roman pontiffs, since they hold power which is proper to them. . . ."[64] The German episcopate was encouraged by that statement and quoted it in Küng's generation.

60. J. Ridley Stroop, *The Church of the Bible* (Nashville: J. Ridley Stroop, 1962), pp. 99-100.

61. Ibid., pp. 100-101.

62. Lightfoot, *The Apostolic Fathers*, p. 36.

63. G. H. Lang, *The Churches of God* (London: Paternoster, 1959), pp. 13-14.

64. Hans Küng, *Structures of the Church*, trans. Salvator Attanasio (New York: Nelson, 1964), pp. 236-37.

When dealing with the question of scriptural guidelines for congregations cooperating with one another, Lewis Hale insists there are no instances where one church sends money to help support another's preacher or to construct a building. "We allow it on the same principle as help for the poor."[65] (See Rom. 15:26).

Hale identifies six elements of autonomy: control of one's own resources; oversight of one's own work; management of one's own affairs; discipline of one's own disorderly members; ability to care for one's own worthy indigent; and governing one's self in all matters of judgment and expediency.[66]

Radmacher lists six guidelines for measuring the degree of autonomy in a local church. His list insures the church the authority to judge its own membership (1 Cor. 5:12–13); to elect its own officers (Acts 6:1–6); to guard and observe the ordinances (1 Cor. 11:23); to settle its own internal difficulties (1 Cor. 6:1–5); to direct matters involving relations with other local congregations (Acts 15:1–2, 22–23, 25, 30); and to govern its own affairs (Matt. 18:17). He closes by saying, "There is no higher court."[67]

One factor to be considered when discussing autonomy is to evaluate where an organization is in its history. C. Peter Wagner indicates that as a mission is planted and matures, the relationship between parent and offspring changes from that of control, to one as guide, and finally as consultant.[68]

Perhaps the most helpful aid to this whole discussion of autonomy is a chart by William R. Read, Victor M. Monterroso, and Harmon A. Johnson. This illustration has obvious parallels to the issue of congregational, presbyterial, and episcopal relations in the development of the church. Interestingly, the increased tendency to maintain control of churches by bishops in church history is reversed in this chart. The chart (table 11) may be interpreted, however, as how the process ought to be rather than how it is.

Radmacher distinguishes four different varieties of bishops in history. First, the bishop of the New Testament is the same as a pastor, elder, and presbyter. Second, pastors of large churches became known as monarchal bishops since fellow elders were willing to be under their

65. Lewis Hale, *How Churches Can Cooperate* (Austin: Firm Foundation Publishing House, n.d.) pp. 43–44.

66. Ibid., pp. 77–81.

67. Radmacher, *What the Church Is All About*, pp. 346–48.

68. C. Peter Wagner, *Frontiers of Missionary Strategy* (Chicago: Moody, 1971), p. 176.

Table 11  **Autonomy and Stages of Church Development**

|  | Stage of Church Development | | | | |
| --- | --- | --- | --- | --- | --- |
| Mission relationship | Pioneer | Emerging Church | Cooperation | Beginning Autonomy | Final Autonomy |
| Outsider | Apostolate | | | | |
| Outside Control | | Administrator | | | |
| Integral Part of National Growth | | | Partner | | |
| Invited Ministry | | | | Servant | |
| Agent of Inter-Church Ministry | | | | | Consultant |

Taken from William R. Read, Victor M. Monterroso, and Harmon A. Johnson, *Latin American Church Growth* (Grand Rapids: Eerdmans, 1969), p. 292. Used by permission.

authority. This was often to provide security and social strength during times of intense persecution. Third, as persecution and time passed, the churches were given legal status by emperors in the fourth century. Constantine, as emperor, led in organizing the church into provinces, after the model of the Roman Empire. Metropolitan bishops served as religious governors over these areas. Finally, papal supremacy as advocated by Irenaeus developed.[69]

The analysis of John Cunningham in his classic, *The Growth of the Church*, is worthy of consideration.[70] The history of the church is seen as evolving through the five phases of individualism, congregationalism, presbyterianism, episcopalianism, and papalism. Each is understood to coexist with the others as the progression develops.

The era of individualism corresponds to Jesus' public and private ministries. Congregationalism is seen as commencing with the churches in Acts and the selection of seven men for ministry (Acts 6). The books of Galatians and Romans are seen as calling for individual decision in the context of community (Rom. 14:4–5). "Thus then, in the bosom of this type of Congregationalism there already existed the germ of a future Episcopacy."[71]

By presbyterianism is meant government by presbyters (i.e., pastors, elders). Cunningham confesses that along the path of history "there are always lost links. The same thing can be said of Christian development. The first form of Presbyterianism was congregational. It is curious we

69. Radmacher, *What the Church Is All About*, p. 50.
70. John Cunningham, *The Growth of the Church* (London: Macmillan, 1886), pp. 8–76.
71. Ibid., pp. 22–23.

have no account of the first institution of presbyters in the Church."[72] He mentions that all early synagogues had elders and suggests that the earliest form of presbyterianism might well have been established by a synagogue whose members became Christians but maintained this existing form of organization. "Presbyter," he notes, is the term used by Jewish converts and "bishops" the term used by Greek converts. By the end of the first century, the presbyterial rule by pastors in the churches was well established.

The beginning of the second century marked the appearance of the episcopalian organizational pattern. Again, Cunningham stresses that "at no period do we find any one of the rival polities altogether disentangled from the others."[73]

> By Episcopacy I do not mean government by bishops, for there were bishops from the beginning, but a polity which insists upon the necessity of a three-fold and three-graded ministry—bishops, presbyters, and deacons—and which assigns to bishops jurisdiction over presbyters and powers of ordination which presbyters do not possess.[74]

Cunningham notes that it was not until the third century that the idea of bishops occupying the place of the apostles began to be popular. Soon after that they even claimed authority to forgive sins. He refers to the reasons for the rise of the episcopacy given by J. B. Lightfoot, who relied on the writings of Ignatius (110), Irenaeus (180), and Cyprian (250). "The church was plunged in a sea of trouble—heathenism without, heresy within—and it was necessary there should be unity and authority, and this the episcopate provided."[75]

Congregational episcopacy, one bishop for each church, was practiced by Patrick (389–461), reports Cunningham. Patrick is reported to have ordained 365 bishops for 365 churches, as well as 3,000 presbyters.[76]

> When diocesan episcopacy appeared, congregational independency perished.... As the bishop rose above the presbyter, the metropolitan rose above the bishop, the patriarch above the metropolitan, and at last the Pope, or universal bishop, crowned the whole. The ecclesiastical map

72. Ibid., pp. 24–25.
73. Ibid., p. 33.
74. Ibid., p. 33.
75. Ibid., p. 59.
76. Ibid., p. 66.

was framed after the civil one. For the Roman empire was at that time divided into fourteen political dioceses, and these were subdivided into a hundred and eighteen provinces, and these into an almost countless number of parishes. The bishop had charge of a ... parish, the metropolitan had charge of a ... province, and the patriarch had charge of a ... diocese.[77]

"No church," concludes Cunningham, "has a divine right to the exclusion of all others. That church has the divinest right which does its work the best ... the Church ... can thus be accommodated to every country and every age."[78]

If Cunningham is correct that "no church has a divine right to the exclusion of others," this means that tradition takes precedence over Scripture as the basic blueprint for all churches, parent and satellite. Varieties of the same conclusion are held by Read, Monterroso, and Johnson, Arthur P. Stanley, and Gene A. Getz.[79] Opposing his conclusion are Kuen, Augustus H. Strong, and Alexander R. Hay.[80] According to Kuen, this latter view is also supported by Lang.[81]

Read, Monterroso, and Johnson feel confident that

in the final analysis it is not so much the form of church government that determines the effectiveness of the Church. Rather, it is upon the shoulders of those in authority—those who are the decisionmakers ... that the responsibility to inspire, influence and orient the entire Church rests.[82]

They illustrate their claim with Pentecostals in Latin America who seem to thrive and adapt in any governmental climate. "The key to their growth is this dynamic, incorporated in an ecclesiastical structure at the local level."[83]

77. Ibid., p. 70.
78. Ibid., p. 76.
79. See William R. Read, Victor M. Monterroso, and Harmon A. Johnson, *Latin American Church Growth* (Grand Rapids: Eerdmans, 1969), pp. 288-89; Arthur P. Stanley, *The Epistles of St. Paul to the Corinthians* (London: John Murray, 1882), p. 280; Gene A. Getz, *Sharpening the Focus of the Church* (Chicago: Moody, 1974), pp. 82-83, 162.
80. See Kuen, *I Will Build My Church*, p. 272; Augustus H. Strong, *Systematic Theology* (1907; Philadelphia: Judson, 1947), p. 896; Alexander R. Hay, *The New Testament Order for Church and Missionary* (Buenos Aires: SEMCA, 1947), p. 127.
81. Kuen, *I Will Build My Church*, p. 272, citing Lang, *The Churches of God*, p. 33.
82. Read, Monterroso, and Johnson, *Latin American Church Growth*, p. 289.
83. Ibid., pp. 288-89.

Getz insists that the church in our day "must develop its own contemporary forms and structures for applying the biblical principles.... Forms and structures in the Scriptures are presented as a means to biblical ends. In themselves they are not absolute."[84] Elsewhere he says, "It is impossible to derive specific patterns and structures from the New Testament (which is also abundantly demonstrated by the many different types of church government in existence today among evangelical believers)."[85]

Opposing this, Kuen writes,

> The New Testament form of the church is also the one which is the most adaptable to the various geographic, ethnic, and political conditions in which the gospel is called to establish itself among men "out of every tribe and tongue and people and nation (Rom. 5:9)."[86]

Hay concludes, "The fact is that the Apostles ... laid a complete and perfect foundation for the Church, both as regards structure and doctrine."[87]

The concept of the parent church and the satellite chapel can be illustrated by statements from the New Testament:

> Again, the kingdom of heaven is like unto a net, that was cast into the sea, and gathered of every kind. [Matt. 13:47]

> For we being many are one bread, and one body: for we are all partakers of that one bread. [1 Cor. 10:17]

> I am the true vine, and my Father is the husbandman. Every branch in me that beareth not fruit he taketh away: and every branch that beareth fruit, he purgeth it, that it may bring forth more fruit.... I am the vine, ye are the branches: He that abideth in me, and I in him, the same bringeth forth much fruit: for without me ye can do nothing. [John 15:1–2, 5]

> For we are labourers together with God: ye are God's husbandry, ye are God's building. [1 Cor. 3:9]

> And the lord said unto the servant, Go out into the highways and hedges, and compel them to come in, that my house may be filled. [Luke 14:23]

84. Getz, *Sharpening the Focus of the Church*, p. 82.
85. Ibid., p. 167.
86. Kuen, *I Will Build My Church*, p. 272.
87. Hay, *The New Testament Order for Church and Missionary*, p. 127.

Ye also, as lively stones, are built up a spiritual house, an holy priesthood, to offer up spiritual sacrifices, acceptable to God by Jesus Christ. [1 Peter 2:5]

Now ye are the body of Christ, and members in particular. [1 Cor. 12:27]

Through the books of Paul Yonggi Cho and John W. Hurston and his daughter Karen L. Hurston, scriptures relating to multiplication by division into satellite cell groups, the involvement of members in evangelistic and nurture ministries, and the use of homes as centers of multiplication have been explained for those who want to know more.

The Hurstons list six biblical principles or foundations for satellite ministries in the large church. Three of these are mentioned in the previous paragraph.

The principle identified as "Leadership Needs Leadership" is an application of Exodus 18:13-27. In that passage Jethro, Moses' father-in-law, advises him to divide Israel into smaller groups led by godly men. The twenty-first verse reads, "Thou shalt provide out of all the people able men, such as fear God, men of truth, hating covetousness; and place such over them, to be rulers of thousands, and rulers of hundreds, rulers of fifties, and rulers of tens."

"This was to be done for these reasons: 1) in order that Moses would be able to endure (v. 23); 2) in order that Moses would be free to be 'Godward' (v. 19); 3) in order that the people would regain peace and harmony (v. 23)."[88] The Hurstons point out that the selection and appointment of the first seven deacons in Acts 6:1-6 also specifies Godwardness and need for peace.

Second, the principle of "The Lay Leader—A Ministering Servant" focuses on Acts 6:1-8 and 8:40. Ministry, rather than mere honor, is seen as the motive in building servants able to preach, evangelize, pray for and care for the sick, and teach God's Word.

Third, the principle of "Utilization of Women" is pointed to in Romans 16:1 and Acts 18:2-3, 18-19.

Fourth, the principle of "The Home as a Place of Worship" views homes as celebration centers for evangelism and nurture by these fast-growing large churches.

88. John W. Hurston and Karen L. Hurston, *Caught in the Web: The Home Cell Unit System at Full Gospel Central Church, Seoul, Korea* (Seoul: Church Growth International, 1977), pp. 15-16.

The Greek word for house, *oikos*, appears at least nineteen times, with there being nine references to times when believers worshiped and/or were taught in a home (2:2–4; 2:56; 5:42; 10:24–48; 16:25–34; 16:40; 20:17–20; 21:8–14; 28:8–14; 28:30–31.) We therefore see in Acts a blend of worship and teaching both in the formal structure of the temple and synagogue (parallel to our church buildings), and the informal structure of the home.[89]

Other passages relating to "house-to-house" ministry include Acts 2:46–47 and 20:20. Cell groups meet in homes, offices, and factories.

Satellite cell groups are a common feature in many of the largest churches of the world (see table 12).

## An Index of the Validity of the Images

A helpful measurement index has been developed from a simple observation made by J. Robertson McQuilkin. McQuilkin is president of Columbia Bible College and Columbia Graduate School of Mission. In *Measuring the Church Growth Movement*, he provides a threefold classification to evaluate the nature of biblical sources of authority. His three categories are biblical mandate, biblical principle, and extrabiblical principle.

McQuilkin, as he describes the three categories, says,

When we speak of bringing Church Growth theses under the authority of the Word of God, we are looking for three distinct kinds of validity: first, those matters which are clearly prescribed in Scripture; then, matters which, though not clearly prescribed, are required because of clear biblical principle; and, finally, those areas which lack such authority,

Table 12  **Satellite Cell Groups, 1982–1983**

| Church | Number of Satellite Cell Groups |
|---|---|
| *Full Gospel Central, Seoul* | 19,839 |
| *Young Nak Presbyterian, Seoul* | 1,562 |
| *Soong-Eui Methodist, Seoul* | 1,000 |
| *Sung-Nak Baptist, Seoul* | 767 |
| *Quang-Lim Methodist, Seoul* | 750 |
| *Choong-Hyun Presbyterian, Seoul* | 747 |
| *Evangelistic Center, San Salvador* | 200 |

Statistics have been gathered by missionary research teams in these countries.

89. Ibid., p. 21.

having been derived from human experience and insight, but which are nevertheless compatible with biblical teaching.[90]

The broad scope of topics discussed to this point includes the validity of the large church and satellite groups for numerical growth, pastoral care, optimum size of congregations, avoiding carnality, urban evangelism, the danger of distorted doctrine, satellite groups, autonomy, priesthood of believers, and buildings as potential barriers to growth.

The topics best classified under biblical mandate include numerical growth, pastoral care, optimum size, avoiding carnality, urban evangelism, the danger of distorted doctrine, and priesthood of the believers.

Topics best classified as biblical principle are satellite groups, autonomy, and buildings as barriers.

Episcopacy as a system of church government is classified as extrabiblical. Presbyterial structure is allowable by biblical principle and congregationalism by biblical mandate.

Numerical growth is the natural harvest of the shared gospel. Examples of this mandate to reach out to the universal need of "all peoples" to know God and his great salvation are many (e.g., Ps. 67:1–2, 7; 102:22; 117; Isa. 45:22; 49:6; Matt. 18:4; 22:37–40; 28:19–20; Mark 16:15; Luke 15:7, 10; 19:10; 24:47–48; John 3:16; 15:8, 16; 20:21; Acts 1:7–8; 1 Tim. 2:4; 2 Peter 3:9; Rev. 7:9; 17:14).

The mandate for pastoral care dominates the message of the New Testament in the "one-another" passages (see p. 29, n. 25). Acts 6 illustrates how growth can result in "neglect" and "murmuring." The biblical command to remove the spiritual unemployment problem of the church through mobilizing members to use their spiritual gifts is clearly explained in Romans 12, 1 Corinithinas 12, and Ephesians 4.

The principle of optimum size proposes that through the use of small groups a church can experience unlimited growth. Unlimited, however, implies that at some point, as in the case of the Jerusalem church (Acts 8:1, 4; 11:19), subdividing of larger groups becomes essential (Rev. 7:9; 17:14). Passages like Jeremiah 33:3, Ephesians 3:20–21, Hebrews 1:1, and 1 John 5:14–15 suggest that we ought to let God set his own limits on what he wants to do through his Holy Spirit and his people.

The command to avoid carnality, especially pride and untamed

90. J. Robertson McQuilkin, *Measuring the Church Growth Movement: Is It Biblical?* (Chicago: Moody, 1974), p. 13.

ambition, is repeated throughout Scripture (1 Peter 5:3; Luke 22:24–27).

Urban evangelism was on the heart and in the mind of Jesus (Luke 4:43; 19:41). Cho comments, "Being satisfied with smallness not only reveals to me a lack of insight, but also a lack of compassion. With three billion people still awaiting the opportunity to reject or accept the gospel, this is no time to be self-satisfied."[91] The seven letters of Revelation 2–3 were written to urban churches. Jerusalem, Antioch, Athens, Corinth, Rome, and Ephesus were urban centers that became targets of the gospel for Jesus, Peter, and Paul.

Distortion of doctrine and scriptural cautions against it are real. This is a constant threat to any church, but especially the large, fast-growing church without "leadership for leaders" (Matt. 5:19; 15:9; 1 Tim. 1:7; 4:2; 6:3; 2 Tim. 4:3; Titus 1:11; 2 Peter 2:1).

The principle of satellite groups is rooted in the example of dividing large groups for more effective ministry. Examples can be found in Moses' division of Israel (Exodus 18), Jesus' selection of the twelve to multiply his own ministry (Matthew 10:1), the sending out of the seventy evangelists in pairs (Luke 10), the selection of seven deacons, the feeding of the 4,000 and 5,000 by smaller groups (Matthew 14–15), and ministry from "house to house" (Acts 2:46–47; 20:20). God early speaks to Abraham in terms of groups of people (Gen. 18:18; 22:18; 28:14).

Many passages about autonomy have already been cited. First Peter 5:3 warns God's people against lording over God's heritage. First Corinthians 12 reminds the believer to be careful to honor the uniqueness of his brother's ministry. Also, each church in Revelation 2–3 was accountable directly to God for its ministry.

Buildings as barriers was never a major problem in the New Testament because the "house-to-house" principle was honored and practiced.

91. Paul Yonggi Cho with R. Whitney Manzano, *More Than Numbers* (Waco: Word, 1984), p. 18.

# 4

## Satellite Models
## in Three Churches

Churches start and stop growing for a variety of reasons. In this chapter we will review selected reasons for each. A comparative evaluation of three large churches with satellite groups will also be given.

### Factors That Influence Church Growth

J. Robertson McQuilkin illustrates growth of a church by five figures used in the Bible. The five elements are weather, representing the sovereignty and activity of God; seed, representing the content of our communication (the Word of God); sower as the communicator and witness; the soil as receiver of the communication; and sowing as the method of communication.[1]

Growth of the churches in the 1970s was marked by the rise of large "shopping center type churches with their multiple services to members."[2] Hollis L. Green comments,

1. J. Robertson McQuilkin, *Measuring the Church Growth Movement: Is It Biblical?* (Chicago: Moody, 1974), pp. 56–57.
2. Elmer L. Towns, *Is the Day of the Denomination Dead?* (Nashville: Nelson, 1973), p. 133.

Generally, "slow growth indicates that something is wrong with the quality of life in the church...." There is abundant evidence around the world in Brazil, in Chile, in Indonesia and in Latin America that rapid growth continues to be the norm for the New Testament congregations.[3]

To the outsider there appears to be a mystique about the astonishing growth many of the larger churches are undergoing today. As a participant in the large-church movement, Elmer L. Towns lists five reasons for having the large church:

1. The large church is biblical and reflects the numerical growth in the book of Acts (Acts 1:21; Acts 2:41; Acts 4:4; Acts 5:14, 28, 42; Acts 6:1, 7). The emphasis on large numbers in the book of Acts allows for a local church to be large.
2. The large church is able to evangelize the entire metropolitan area.
3. The large church provides all of the spiritual gifts to the local church.
4. The large church can be a conscience to the community and speak out against the social issues in the community.
5. The large church replaces the necessity for a denomination. There are four basic services that a denomination gives to a small local church ... fellowship ... program for outreach ... finances for loans ... literature.... The large church can provide all of these four services within its local church organization, hence ruling out the need for a denomination.[4]

The large church of today is able to reach beyond its own neighborhood to an entire city. Cultural barriers are easier to cross, especially with satellite groups, because ethnic communities can maintain their cultural identities as they are encouraged to evangelize within their own cultural context. Or, other ethnic groups can be incorporated into the life of the larger church. The large congregation is better able to develop a wide variety of ministries to meet a greater variety of needs.

3. Hollis L. Green, *Why Churches Die: A Guide to Basic Evangelism and Church Growth* (Minneapolis: Bethany Fellowship, 1972), p. 95.
4. Elmer L. Towns, *America's Fastest Growing Churches: Why Ten Sunday Schools Are Growing Fast* (Nashville: Impact Books, 1972), pp. 190–91.

East Hill Church in Gresham, Oregon, grew to over forty-five hundred members by 1979. They wanted to construct a building in which the entire congregation could worship together without drawing their members' giving away from the support of their extensive programs in ministry. Their solution? They established a separate corporation to build a self-supporting convention center, which the church uses free.[5]

Large churches with satellite groups are able to reach an urban area through small groups. Howard A. Snyder notes, "The small group is not a panacea. . . . But the small group is an essential component of the church's structure and life."[6]

Snyder is convinced that "normal growth comes by the division of cells, not by the unlimited expansion of existing cells. The growth of individual cells beyond a certain point without division is pathological."[7]

Church growth research would seem to suggest . . . that once a congregation has grown to a few hundred members the rate of growth will slow down unless new branch congregations are formed through growth by division. Where notable exceptions to this pattern are found, closer examination will usually reveal that the local "congregation" running into the thousands is in reality a whole network of smaller "subcongregations" in which growth by division is taking place as the normal pattern.[8]

Numerous causes can lead to the decline of a congregation. One reason, which is sociologically rooted, is the problem of second-generation sect leadership. H. Richard Niebuhr has written, "By its very nature the sectarian type of organization is valid only for one generation. . . . Rarely does a second generation hold the convictions it has inherited with a fervor equal to that of its fathers. . . ."[9]

Niebuhr warns that as a religious group becomes more "formal and ethically harmless" it separates itself from its unique usefulness to the masses. If a leader is not raised up within the group to lead a new

5. Tom Sine, *The Mustard Seed Conspiracy: You Can Make a Difference in Tomorrow's Troubled World* (Waco: Word, 1981), p. 176.

6. Howard A. Snyder, *The Problem of Wine Skins: Church Structure in a Technological Age* (Downers Grove: Inter-Varsity, 1975), p. 147.

7. Howard A. Snyder, *The Community of the King* (Downers Grove: Inter-Varsity, 1977), p. 123.

8. Ibid.

9. H. Richard Niebuhr, *The Social Sources of Denominationalism* (1929; New York: Meridian, 1957), pp. 19-20.

movement back to its roots, "the secularization of the masses and the transfer of their religious fervor to secular movements, which hold some promise of salvation from the evils that afflict them, is the probable result."[10] He indicates that this is exactly what has happened to presbyterian churches as "sermons were not only unintelligible ... [but also] irrelevant. The whole trend of the day was against any second-hand religion [among the masses] ... the disinherited required an emotionally experienceable and expressible faith...."[11]

Doctrine can become a hindrance to growth, as J. B. A. Kessler, Jr., indicates in his study of Protestants in Peru and Chile. He says they misapply their external security for early social security and forget that although works do not save, the saved do work. As a result, Pentecostals with a different theology of eternal security were "less prone to become supremely satisfied with their own salvation. This was an important factor in the development of their lay ministry."[12]

Buildings, as mentioned earlier, can be a barrier to growth. If the church can grow only as fast as buildings, budgets, and ordained staff can be provided, growth will be hindered once it begins.

Failure of members and potential members to become involved in small "face-to-face" and "heart-to-heart" groups, to use C. Peter Wagner's terms, can seriously hinder and even halt growth. Gordon MacDonald notes,

> When someone says, "The church is getting so large I don't know everyone," the answer is simple. "No one has to know everyone; just make sure you are a member of a subcongregation. No one can relate to more than forty or fifty people ... and the subcongregational structure allows for relationships within a large church." The Jerusalem church was obviously a large church, and its subcongregations met "from house to house...."[13]

He continues, "Leaders perceived as lacking warmth can hinder growth in a church. This condition begins with the pastor.... Growing churches must find ways to break people down into small groups ... where immediate attention can be given.... Growth demands it."[14]

10. Ibid., pp. 31–32.

11. Ibid., p. 43.

12. J. B. A. Kessler, Jr., "Hindrances to Church Growth," *International Review of Missions*, July 1968, p. 301.

13. Gordon MacDonald, "Ten Conditions for Church Growth," *Leadership*, Winter 1983, p. 46.

14. Ibid., p. 48.

Sometimes all that is needed is "great growth" to move a church from its present plateau. Donald A. McGavran encouragingly reminds us, "We are called to create a ministry which will keep growing churches growing and start now—growing churches on the road to great growth."[15]

One research project by Wagner and Richard L. Gorsuch identified the multiplication of fellowship groups to be highly correlated to growing churches as opposed to declining churches.

Declining churches gave a 5.8 rating to fellowship, while growing churches put it around 7.2.... Growing churches put a higher priority on this than nongrowing churches. But which is the cause and which the effect? Does growth create fellowship, or does fellowship create growth?[16]

Another reason for decline is loss of doctrinal distinctiveness by a group. Towns reveals that liberal theology is a definite deterrent to growth. He ranks the rate of growth among fundamentalist, evangelical, and liberal or mainline denominationalism from fastest to slowest in that order. "Numerical growth reflects the theological and sociological posture of the church's position on the sociological cycle."[17]

Lack of an abundance of trained leaders can cause major halting of growth:

Examination of rapidly growing churches ... affords substantiation of the principle ... upon concerned Christians everywhere: a major secret of power and of church growth is the recruiting and training of large numbers of people for responsible places of leadership in the congregation.[18]

Much more could be said about the causes of growth and decline in churches. William R. Read, Victor M. Monterroso, and Harmon A. Johnson reduce growth and nongrowth to three criteria: right location, right message, and right suppositions.

Right location refers, for example, to focusing attention on receptive

15. Donald A. McGavran, *How Churches Grow* (London: World Dominion, 1957), p. 142.

16. C. Peter Wagner and Richard L. Gorsuch, "The Quality Church (Part 1)," *Leadership*, Winter 1983, p. 31.

17. Towns, *America's Fastest Growing Churches*, p. 156.

18. Neil Braun, *Laity Mobilized: Reflections on Church Growth in Japan and Other Lands* (Grand Rapids: Eerdmans, 1971), pp. 81-82

populations rather than concentrating all of a mission's efforts on reaching a group that is resistant to the gospel. Read, Monterroso, and Johnson also caution against being bound by outdated comity arrangements or working exclusively with small target groups. They further mention that missionaries often concentrate on working with churches that cannot sustain themselves financially. A broader base is needed, the authors note.

Preaching the right message means insuring indigeneity in worship forms. It also includes dealing with people in their cultural context, knowing their language, and using metaphors that they will understand. The authors also urge that missionaries not be bound to developing institutions (e.g., hospitals) or promoting ecclesiastical structures that are used in North America.

Right suppositions are valid priorities concerning institutions and methodology. The mix of these ingredients must often, in the authors' opinion, help or halt growth.[19]

Other contributing factors influencing growth and nongrowth include group structural imbalance, faith and expectancy, and realization that revival or renewal does not necessarily guarantee numerical growth.

## Three Churches with Satellite Groups

The satellite concept involves the whole issue of church planting or starting new churches.

One of the simplest but most helpful outlines of the various methods of beginning new churches is given by the Nazarene writer Paul R. Orjala in *Get Ready to Grow*.[20] He discusses nine methods of planting new congregations, one of which is the satellite method. For a detailed report on these methods, see chapter 6 of his book.

The nine models Orjala evaluates include what he calls parenting, satellite, multicongregational, brothering, colonization, district team, catalytic, fusion, and task force. Figure 1 is a graphic adaptation of those nine models. The circles indicate the relationship of churches and small groups. Circles of larger or equal size represent regularly constituted churches. The smaller circles symbolize small groups related to the larger congregation or congregations.

19. William R. Read, Victor H. Monterroso, and Harmon A. Johnson, *Latin American Church Growth* (Grand Rapids: Eerdmans, 1969), pp. 302–11.

20. Paul R. Orjala, *Get Ready to Grow* (Kansas City, Mo.: Beacon Hill, 1978), pp. 108–15.

Figure 1 **Nine Models of How Churches Relate in Church Planting**

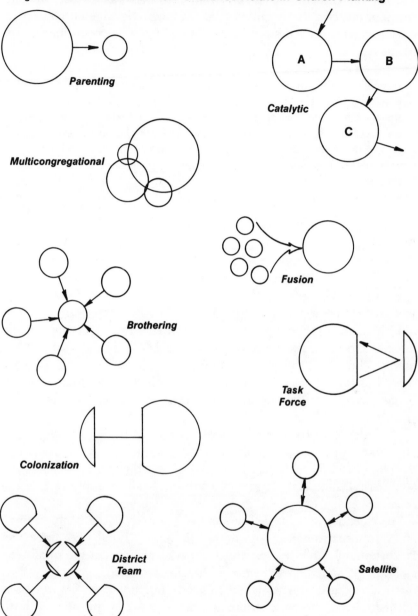

Diagrams are by John N. Vaughan and are based on the descriptions by Paul R. Orjala, *Get Ready to Grow* (Kansas City, Mo.: Beacon Hill, 1978), pp. 108–15.

The three churches being compared in this chapter all have satellite-group ministries. Each church has adapted the satellite concept to reflect its own priorities and preferences. Orjala describes the satellite model as

> a version of the parenting model that is probably the most widespread plan used today by growing churches and movements around the world. Its value lies in the fact that it combines in its method the growth of the parent church by expansion and the potential for planting a new church as a result of its success. It is a model in which the local church gains a good part of its expansion growth through the multiplication of outreach groups in the neighborhoods of its members.... When these groups grow, the local church grows—but also the outreach groups at a distance may become house churches with the future potential of full church organization. The satellite model multiplies the opportunity for lay leadership development. Some may sense a call to full-time ministry and continue on as pastors of the new churches when they are organized.[21]

For the present purposes, one more figure is necessary to distinguish the basic differences in the approach used by the three churches. Four models of the satellite concept are shown (see fig. 2). The traditional satellite group is designated S-1. The satellite is an extension of the mother church and is designed to grow and become an independent church at some later date. This model is called the traditional transitional satellite model. Each of the three churches has begun new churches with this method.

The extended dependent satellite model (S-2) is like S-1 except that often there are multiple groups. The intention of the parent group is to maintain them for an indefinite, extended period of time. The Jotabeche Methodist Pentecostal Church of Santiago is an example of this approach.

The extended satellite cell model (S-3) represents the simplest form of cell-ministry satellites. Both Yoido Full Gospel Church and Young Nak Presbyterian Church began with this model. Notice that the small cells labeled $P$ (parent) have their own daughter cells (the dark circles). At this early stage, larger satellite mission churches have not yet been formed. This is the basic distinction between S-3, a transitional form, and S-4.

The preliminary stage for the development of a new fully constituted

21. Ibid., pp. 109–10.

Figure 2 **Basic Satellite-Group Structures**

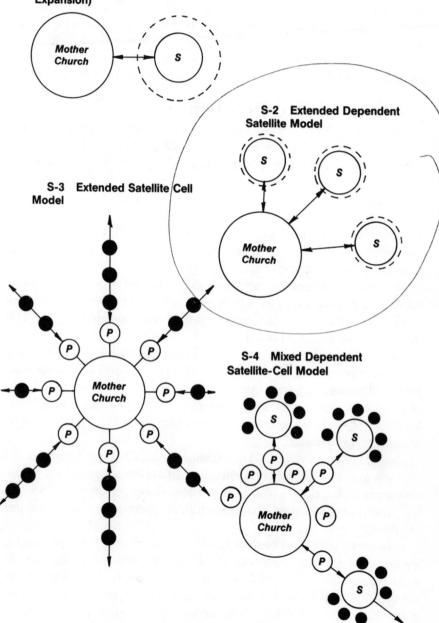

**S-1   Traditional Transitional Satellite Model (Extension-Expansion)**

Mother Church

S

**S-2   Extended Dependent Satellite Model**

S

S

S

Mother Church

**S-3   Extended Satellite Cell Model**

P
P
P
P
P
P
P
P

Mother Church

**S-4   Mixed Dependent Satellite-Cell Model**

S

S

P

P   P   P

P

Mother Church

P

S

church is S-4. The mother church determines if the satellite mission church (S) and cells it is parenting itself will remain dependent or will be allowed to become a fully autonomous congregation with its own satellite network.

Information on each of these three churches was gathered from use of the questionnaire found in Appendix A, on-site observation, a missionary research team, and interviews. All information about these churches is available in detail in *The World's Twenty Largest Churches*.

### *Jotabeche Methodist Pentecostal Church*

Santiago, a city of almost 4,000,000 people, has a population equal to half that of Moscow or Seoul, but is larger than Berlin, Rome, or Jerusalem. Chile's territory in square miles slightly exceeds that of Texas.

Two million people, about one-sixth of the total population of Chile, are evangelicals. Pentecostals make up 90 percent of the evangelical population and one-third of all Pentecostals are identified with the Methodist Pentecostal church. The Jotabeche Church is both the largest Methodist Pentecostal church and the largest Christian church in Chile. It is the second largest church in the world.

The membership of the mother church, reported to be 80,000 people, excludes all children under age twelve. Actual membership probably exceeds 100,000. The congregation reported 800 baptisms in 1980. The auditorium seats 15,000 people.

The congregation ministers to Santiago through a network of forty temples (the capacity of each exceeds 600 people) and sixty preaching points called locales (capacity of each is fewer than 600 persons). These satellite locations are as far as ten miles from the main temple on Jotabeche Street in the heart of downtown Santiago. The satellite groups are also called annexes.

Each Monday and Thursday worship services are conducted in the annexes in the neighborhoods. All annex members are members of the mother church. Friday night of each week a large celebration service at the main temple, called the cathedral, is open to members of the satellites.

Because of the broad base of members, the church has developed a system whereby only one-fourth of the annexes attend the main temple each Sunday. This is scheduled with the annexes by their location in the city. The city is divided into four sections and each section rotates attendance with the other three sections. Each section is allowed to attend only one Sunday each month.

The thunder of praise fills the concrete and wood sanctuary when it is filled. The simple wooden pews equipped with moveable kneeling benches add to the simplicity of the service.

Street-evangelism teams from the church are familiar sights throughout the city. The pastor is the only person authorized to baptize. Five hundred volunteers preach in the streets of Santiago each Monday. They also meet each Tuesday before going to visit hospitals, jails, and prisons. They all preach somewhere every Monday in Santiago. Also, all teachers at both the main temple and the satellite locations are taught each week at the main temple. Pastor Javier Vasqrez indicates that approximately three new chapels are begun each year. During his first seventeen years as pastor, ten men leading the larger chapels have been ordained and their temples released by the mother church as independent congregations.

### Yoido Full Gospel Church

Pastored by Paul Yonggi Cho, Yoido Full Gospel Church is the largest and also the most researched church in the world. The congregation began on May 18, 1958, when 5 members met in a tent church. According to reports in early 1981, about 1 new member was being added every five and a half minutes, or 264 daily. During 1983 the church was adding 10,000 members per month. Sunday-school attendance is about 20,900 persons each week. Leadership at the church includes 523 employees, of whom 316 are ministry staff. In addition, the church operates 3 mission churches in Korea and has planted 118 churches in other countries. Membership exceeded 500,000 in 1985.

Many observers credit the congregation's cell groups with being the major key to the growth of Yoido Full Gospel Church. Leaders within the church, however, stress that the cells are channels of growth rather than the cause for growth. Actually, both elements are probably operational.

Seven levels of leadership have existed in the cell groups since their inception in 1958; adding an eighth level is under consideration. By 1961 the church had 125 cells with a membership of 7,750 (2,267 families). In 1974, three significant decisions were made: the church began printing a weekly outline for Bible students in the cells; the city was divided into twenty-one areas of ministry; and each of these areas was supervised by a member of the pastoral staff.

Cell groups—19,839 of them, each composed of no more than fifteen members—meet, usually on Friday evening, in homes, offices, and factories across Seoul. Each group has a cell leader and an assistant cell leader, many of whom are women. When groups include fifteen members, they divide into two smaller groups, which begin to grow again until each has fifteen members. The process is continual.

### Young Nak Presbyterian Church

Pastor Park Cho Choon has led the Young Nak Presbyterian Church since 1973. He and Han Kyung Chik, the founding pastor, are both graduates of Princeton Theological Seminary.

Young Nak, like Yoido Full Gospel Church, was begun by refugees fleeing the Communist takeover of North Korea.

This 60,000-member church is the largest Presbyterian congregation in the world. Cho, pastor of Yoido Full Gospel Church, recalls when Young Nak was the largest church in Seoul with about 6,000 members. At one point Cho determined that the sanctuary of Young Nak seated more than 2,000 persons. He then decided to build an even larger church.

In 1950 the church had only 27 members and 1 home study group. By 1970 the church had grown to more than 13,000 members with 210 home cell groups and averaged receiving 1 new member daily. Ten years later, the church reported nearly 40,000 members with 673 cell groups. It added an average of 8 new members daily.

At the beginning of 1984 satellite cell groups numbered 1,562 with 56,232 attending each week. Average cell-group attendance is thirty-five members each.

Young Nak's groups have five leaders per cell, each of which is composed of about twelve families. Each cell includes one elder (a layman), one woman exhorter, and three younger women who serve as kwan chal (visitors). These three women visit each family from their cell each week, usually on Friday.

Sunday-school attendance is 12,400. The total number of deacons and deaconesses is 4,000. The church has twenty-five persons on its ministry staff, twenty-five evangelists, and fifty other employees for a total of a hundred paid employees.

Twenty-two new churches were begun by the Young Nak men's and women's missionary society in 1980. Since 1947 nearly 170 satellite churches have been established as autonomous churches. The church in 1984 operates 25 satellite mission churches.

# *Epilogue*

$L$arge churches with satellite groups are obviously not the only churches that are experiencing growth, even rapid growth.

During times of high inflation and economic uncertainty, the large church can be highly vulnerable. Interestingly, most of the kinds of churches discussed in these pages are located in countries with high inflation. Because of the key role of the small group in churches with satellites, models are coming into focus that will provide alternatives. Today, there are more large churches and therefore more churches of size that are increasingly vulnerable.

Donald A. McGavran, quoted in *Guidelines for Urban Church Planting*, reaffirms solutions to several issues raised in these pages. His eight keys to church growth in the cities are the importance of house churches; the role of unpaid lay leaders; the recognition of resistant classes; focus on the responsive; the multiplication of tribe, caste, and language churches; surmounting the property barrier; an intense belief in Christ; and providing the theological base for justice and integrity in society.[1]

The same priorities are restated by Roger S. Greenway in his experience with Free Methodists in Brazil: begin with a clear biblical under-

---

1. Roger S. Greenway, ed., *Guidelines for Urban Church Planting* (Grand Rapids: Baker, 1976), pp. 24–27.

standing of the church; identify people gifted in church planting; avoid placing property before people; concentrate on homes and households; provide a lively, joyous worship experience; and aim for the multiplication of local congregations.[2]

There is no agency better equipped to launch the strategy outlined by McGavran and Greenway than the large church with satellite groups. An aggressive, growing church is most likely to produce quickly the same kind of offspring able to reproduce and function.

This kind of church has the experience, the faith, the vision, the resources, and the opportunities to discover and train people and churches to reproduce highly contagious soul-oriented churches.

Meanwhile, every church can and ought to reexamine the structure, balance, and leadership currently involved in existing small groups. We need to discover how present groups can be improved and new ones created.

2. Ibid., pp. 28–30.

APPENDIX A

# Church-Growth Information

1. Name of congregation _____

2. Mailing address of congregation _____
   _____

3. Location

   City _____ Population _____

   Province _____ Population _____

   State _____ Population _____

   Country _____ Population _____

4. Is this congregation affiliated with a denominational body of similar congregations? ☐ yes ☐ no

   If the answer is yes, give the following information about that group:

   (1) Location and name of national or international central office _____
   _____

(2) The approximate number of congregations and their total membership affiliated with this association, denomination, or group:

Total congregations _____ Total membership _____

5. Name of pastor _____ Age _____

6. If the congregation has a staff of pastors, please indicate the number of ministry staff (full- or part-time) by category of ministry function (i.e., title or job description).

_____

_____

_____

7. Approximate date this congregation was founded _____

8. Please indicate the number of auditorium and/or Christian-education facilities this congregation has met in during the past, those currently being used, and those now being built or proposed.

| Type of Facility | Date Built | Capacity | Cost |
|---|---|---|---|
| (1) _____ | _____ | _____ | _____ = $ _____ |
| (2) _____ | _____ | _____ | _____ = $ _____ |
| (3) _____ | _____ | _____ | _____ = $ _____ |
| (4) _____ | _____ | _____ | _____ = $ _____ |
| (5) _____ | _____ | _____ | _____ = $ _____ |
| (6) _____ | _____ | _____ | _____ = $ _____ |
| (7) _____ | _____ | _____ | _____ = $ _____ |
| (8) _____ | _____ | _____ | _____ = $ _____ |
| (9) _____ | _____ | _____ | _____ = $ _____ |
| (10) _____ | _____ | _____ | _____ = $ _____ |

9. History of pastors serving the congregation

(1) Total number of senior pastors serving the congregation since it was founded _____

(2) How long has the present pastor served this church? _____ years

(3) List all known pastors who have served this congregation.

|  | Name | Age Now | Years Served |
|---|---|---|---|
| (1) | _____ | _____ | 19 ___ to 19 ___ |
| (2) | _____ | _____ | 19 ___ to 19 ___ |
| (3) | _____ | _____ | 19 ___ to 19 ___ |
| (4) | _____ | _____ | 19 ___ to 19 ___ |
| (5) | _____ | _____ | 19 ___ to 19 ___ |
| (6) | _____ | _____ | 19 ___ to 19 ___ |
| (7) | _____ | _____ | 19 ___ to 19 ___ |
| (8) | _____ | _____ | 19 ___ to 19 ___ |
| (9) | _____ | _____ | 19 ___ to 19 ___ |
| (10) | _____ | _____ | 19 ___ to 19 ___ |

(4) How many churches has the present pastor served? _____

10. Statistical information

Note about information needed: The terms *main* church and *other* churches refer to a group of one or more chapels, missions, or "daughter" churches located away from the main church but still obligated financially and governed by that main congregation. If the church being studied does not have other churches or chapels governed by it or under its financial supervision, you should provide information under items designated main church.

| | Location | 1982 | 1981 | 1980 | 1970 | 1960 | 1950 | 1940 | |
|---|---|---|---|---|---|---|---|---|---|
| Church Members | *Main* | | | | | | | | |
| | *Other* | | | | | | | | |
| Worship Attendance | *Main* | | | | | | | | |
| | *Other* | | | | | | | | |
| Average Sunday-School Attendance | *Main* | | | | | | | | |
| | *Other* | | | | | | | | |
| Sunday-School Enrollment | *Main* | | | | | | | | |
| | *Other* | | | | | | | | |
| Baptisms | *Main* | | | | | | | | |
| | *Other* | | | | | | | | |
| Total Teaching Units | *Main* | | | | | | | | |
| | *Other* | | | | | | | | |
| Total Home Bible-Study Groups | | | | | | | | | |
| Total Offering (in dollars) | | | | | | | | | |
| Households in Total Church (estimate) | | | | | | | | | |

11. Deacon information

    (1) How many active deacons (total)? Main _____Other _____

    (2) Are they organized to minister to families or are they a policy-making board? Explain _____

_____

    (3) Are they elected by the congregation or appointed? Explain _____

_____

    (4) Does the church have deaconesses? _____How many? _____

    (5) In the language of the people, what is the name for

        Pastor _____ Deacon _____

12. Christian-education information

    (1) Is more than one version of the Bible used? Which? _____

_____

    (2) Is a Sunday-school curriculum used officially by the church? \_\_\_\_\_

_____

        Explain _____

_____

_____

    (3) If a curriculum is used, is it produced within the church or by a publishing house? Which publisher? What languages? _____

_____

_____

    (4) If a curriculum is used, is it graded? How? _____

_____

_____

_____

    (5) Is more than one language used in the curriculum or Bibles? Explain

_____

_____

_____

(6)  Do men and women meet in sex-segregated teaching units? _____

_____

(7)  Do boys and girls meet together for study? Give ages _____

_____

_____

(8)  How are teaching units organized?

| Age Groups | Location* | Approximate Attendance | Age of Groups | Approximate Number of Pupils Per Teacher | Total Number of Teachers |
|---|---|---|---|---|---|
| Preschool | Main | | | | |
| | Other | | | | |
| Children | Main | | | | |
| | Other | | | | |
| Youth | Main | | | | |
| | Other | | | | |
| Adult | Main | | | | |
| | Other | | | | |
| TOTAL | | | | | |

* *Other location* means chapels, missions, or daughter churches owned, operated, or supervised by the main or mother congregation.

13.  Indicate the geographical location of the main facility in the city (e.g., northeast, south central, inner city) by a plus sign (+) on the square.

Indicate type of community around the church.
___ High population density (Estimate _____)
___ Moderate population density (Estimate _____)
___ Low population density (Estimate _____)
___ Inner city

___ Suburb

14. Describe a worship service (with outline of order of service with estimated time frames for each portion) at the church (type instruments, choirs, size of choir, colors, etc.).

_____

_____

_____

_____

_____

_____

_____

_____

_____

_____

_____

_____

_____

15. Describe a Bible-study meeting of the church (location, size, and age of group; topic and text of lesson; age, sex, and training of teacher; teaching method; how crowded; sounds; scents; were Bibles used by all; schedule used; singing; time of day or night; day of week).

_____

_____

_____

_____

_____

_____

_____

_____

_____

_____

_____

_____

_____

_____

16. Describe the pastor of the church (height, weight, color of eyes, hair, rate of speech, formal training, temperament, dress, interests or hobbies, favorite text and books of the Bible, favorite doctrine, personal and church goals, views on preaching, evangelism, music).

_____

_____

_____

_____

_____

_____

_____

_____

_____

_____

_____

_____

_____

Number of brothers and sisters _____

Number of sons and daughters _____

Age at conversion _____

Religious background of parents _____

Age began preaching _____

17. Describe the community around the church (be as specific as possible).

_____

_____

_____

_____

_____

_____

_____

_____

_____

_____

_____

_____

_____

_____

_____

_____

18. Mark an *X* by the answer that best describes the worship practices of the congregation.

☐ The church is one group meeting under one roof on a weekly basis.

☐ The church is one group meeting under one roof but it does not meet weekly (explain).

☐ The church is a mother church that meets under one roof each week and has daughter churches or chapels that assemble under their own roofs for a common weekly celebration (explain).

☐ The church is a mother church that meets under one roof each week and has daughter churches that assemble under their own roofs for a common celebration, but they do not meet together weekly (explain).

NOTE: If the mother-church model is used by this church, do the daughter churches have their own pastors? _____ yes _____ no _____ some _____ most

How large is the largest participating daughter church?

_____

Approximately how many daughter churches are there?

_____

How far away from the mother church is the farthest daughter church or chapel? _____ miles

19. Describe the ecumenical attitudes of the church.

_____

_____

_____

_____

20. Describe the doctrinal distinctives of the congregation (what do they put their focus on?). How do they differ from Southern Baptists? What do they believe about baptism, Lord's Supper, conversion, age of conversion, mode of baptism, church officers, spiritual gifts, priorities of the church, membership requirements?

_____

_____

_____

_____

_____

21. Approximately how many members participate in or support the churches' visitation and evangelistic activities each week (percentage or an estimated number)? _____

22. How many estimated soul-winners are there in the church? _____

23. Approximately what percentage of the total baptisms during the past year were new believers? _____

24. How are soul-winners trained by the church?

_____

_____

_____

_____

_____

_____

25. How does the congregation make group decisions? Does it make policy by action of the pastor, deacons, congregation? Does it have regular business meetings as we do in our churches? Does it keep written records or "minutes" as we do in the United States?

_____

_____

_____

_____

_____

_____

26. How are new members oriented into the life of the church? Are members excluded? Is there a waiting period before the new member is baptized?

_____

_____

_____

_____

_____

NOTE: If at all possible supply a photo of the pastor, the building of the church, the congregation, the neighborhood and the city, and a map of the city. Any printed or published histories or articles about the church would be helpful.

27. To what does the pastor attribute the growth of the congregation (i.e., principles or factors)?

    1. _____

       _____

    2. _____

       _____

    3. _____

       _____

    4. _____

       _____

    5. _____

       _____

    6. _____

       _____

    7. _____

       _____

    8. _____

       _____

    9. _____

       _____

28. What is the key Scripture verse the church or pastor may have identified as the promise verse for the congregation? _____

29. Does the church have a logo or motto (e.g., the dove or "nothing is impossible") that it uses to distinguish itself from other churches? _____

    _____

    _____

**Number of churches, resident members, and average attendance of all denominations represented in the area of _____ Church**

| Denominations | Number of Churches | Number of Resident Members | Average Weekly Attendance[a] |
|---|---|---|---|
| Totals | | | |
| | | | |
| Southern Baptists | | | |
| | | | |
| Other Baptists | | | |
| Assembly of God | | | |
| Christian | | | |
| Church of Christ | | | |
| Church of God | | | |
| Congregational | | | |
| Episcopal | | | |
| Jewish | | | |
| Lutheran | | | |
| Methodist | | | |
| Nazarene | | | |
| Pentecostal | | | |
| Presbyterian | | | |
| Roman Catholic | | | |
| Others | | | |
| | | | |
| | | | |
| | | | |

[a]Attendance at Sunday or church school or Sunday morning worship service.

## Ministries Offered by the _____ Church, 19 ___

| Ministries | Check year in which these were in effect | | | |
|---|---|---|---|---|
| | 1980 | 1979 | 1978 | 1977 |
| Adult Education | | | | |
| Kindergarten | | | | |
| Literacy Classes | | | | |
| Job Training | | | | |
| Tutoring Services | | | | |
| Library Services | | | | |
| Preschool Care | | | | |
| Before-After-School Care | | | | |
| Adult Day Care (Sr.) | | | | |
| Short-Time Care | | | | |
| Clothing Distribution | | | | |
| Food Distribution | | | | |
| Medical Clinics | | | | |
| Legal Assistance | | | | |
| Counseling or Referral Service | | | | |
| Teen Club | | | | |
| Mature Adult Club | | | | |
| Scouts | | | | |
| Migrants | | | | |
| Juvenile Delinquents | | | | |
| Alcoholics | | | | |
| College Students | | | | |
| International Groups | | | | |
| Language Groups (Name:        ) | | | | |
| Negroes | | | | |
| Deaf Ministry | | | | |
| Ex-prisoner and Family | | | | |
| Visitation in Church Community | | | | |
| Convalescent Homes | | | | |
| Jail Ministry | | | | |
| Church-Type Missions | | | | |
| Bible-Study Fellowships | | | | |
| Bus Ministry | | | | |

# Church-Growth Models

1. Dan Baumann, *All Originality Makes a Dull Church* (Santa Ana: Calif.: Vision House, 1976).

   (1) Soul-Winning Church
   (2) Classroom Church
   (3) Life-Situation Church
   (4) Social-Action Church
   (5) General-Practitioner Church

2. F. W. Dillistone, *The Structure of the Divine Society* (Philadelphia: Westminster, 1951), pp. 147–216.

   (1) Monastic
   (2) Imperial
   (3) Organic
   (4) Covenantal
   (5) Contractual
   (6) Sectarian

3. Francis M. DuBose, *How Churches Grow in an Urban World* (Nashville: Broadman, 1978), pp. 59–69.

   (1) The Cathedral
   (2) Downtown "Old First"
   (3) Uptown Church
   (4) People's Church
   (5) University Church
   (6) Large Neighborhood Church
   (7) Medium-Size Neighborhood Church
   (8) Small Neighborhood Church
   (9) Storefront Church
   (10) Black Church
   (11) Ethnic Church
   (12) Suburban Church

4. Francis M. DuBose, *How Churches Grow in an Urban World* (Nashville: Broadman, 1978), pp. 83–93.

(1) Regional Church
(2) Rural-Urban-Fringe Church
(3) Megachurch
(4) Base-Satellite Church
(5) Federated Church
(6) Multicongregational Church
(7) Multiethnic Church

(8) Exurban and Rural Church
(9) Ecumenical Church
(10) Relocated Church
(11) Special Purpose Church
(12) Rural Church
(13) Life-Style Church

5. Avery Dulles, *Models of the Church* (Garden City, N.Y.: Doubleday, 1974).

(1) Institution
(2) Mystical Communion
(3) Sacrament

(4) Herald
(5) Servant
(6) Eschatology

6. Gene A. Getz, *The Measure of a Church* (Glendale, Calif.: Regal, 1975), pp. 16–17.

(1) Active Church
(2) Growing Church
(3) Giving Church
(4) Soul-Winning Church

(5) Missionary-Minded Church
(6) Smooth-Running Church
(7) "Spirit-Filled" Church
(8) Big Church

7. Paul R. Orjala, *Get Ready to Grow* (Kansas City, Mo.: Beacon Hill, 1978), pp. 108–15.

(1) Parenting
(2) Satellite
(3) Multi-Congregational
(4) Brothering

(5) Colonization
(6) District Team
(7) Catalytic
(8) Fusion
(9) Task Force

8. James L. Sullivan, *Baptist Polity as I See It* (Nashville: Broadman, 1983), pp. 70–93.

(1) Informal/Unstructured
(2) Independent/Isolationist
(3) Hierarchical

(4) Delegated
(5) Related
(6) Directed/Balanced

9. Elmer L. Towns, John N. Vaughan, and David J. Seifert, *The Complete Book of Church Growth* (Wheaton: Tyndale House, 1981), p. 84.

   (1) Fundamentalism
   (2) Evangelical Bible Church
   (3) Body Life
   (4) Charismatic Renewal
   (5) Southern Baptist
   (6) Mainline Denominational
   (7) Fuller Factor

10. Jerry White, *The Church and the Parachurch: An Uneasy Marriage* (Portland: Multnomah, 1983), p. 77.

    (1) Roman Catholic
    (2) Anglo-Catholic
    (3) Hierarchical (bishops, centralized authority)
    (4) Denominational (elder rule)
    (5) Denominational (congregational rule)
    (6) Associational (elder rule)
    (7) Associational (congregational rule)
    (8) Independent (elder rule)
    (9) Independent (congregational rule)
    (10) Nonstructured House Churches

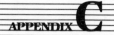

APPENDIX **C**

# Earliest Records
# of Church Building

In the East, beyond the Tigris, evidence of Christian architecture is to be found as early as the second century, for the Chronicle of Arbeia, written by Mesihazekha c. A.D. 550 and based upon the record of Abel (A.D. 171-c. 200), records that the third bishop Isaac (123-36) was responsible for the building of a church. The Chronicle of Edessa also provides the information that there was in the city a templum ecclesiae Christianorum which was destroyed by a flood in A.D. 202. At Dura-Europos on the Euphrates, where the local congregation was not wealthy, a private house was transformed, c. 232, into a Christian place of worship by removing a partition between two rooms and by furnishing another as a baptistry. In Pontus, Gregory Thaumaturgus built a church at Neocaesarea in 258; twelve years later the emperor Aurelian ordered Paul of Samosata to surrender the 'church building' at Antioch to the orthodox party and at the turn of the century Gregory the Illuminator directed the construction of three basilicas at Etchmiadzin. At Nicomedia, the Eastern capital itself, the church was situated on rising ground in full view of the imperial palace, and when Diocletian ordered its destruction it had to be pulled down, as any attempt to fire it would have endangered the surrounding buildings.

In the West, despite the slow spread of Christianity, Tertullian bears witness to the existence of church buildings in the second century, some of them being quite elaborate structures, and after the Peace Constantine gave the clergy of North Africa sufficient money to rebuild those which had been destroyed.

From J. G. Davies, *The Origin and Development of Early Christian Church Architecture* (London: SCM, 1952), pp. 12–15.

# Bibliography

## Books

Allen, Roland. *The Spontaneous Expansion of the Church and the Causes Which Hinder It.* Grand Rapids: Eerdmans, 1962.

Ayer, Joseph Cullen. *A Source Book for Ancient Church History from the Apostolic Age to the Close of the Conciliar Period.* 1913. New York: AMS, 1970.

Banks, Robert J. *Paul's Idea of Community: The Early House Churches in Their Historical Setting.* Grand Rapids: Eerdmans, 1980.

Barnes, Reginald Henry. *Spurgeon: The People's Preacher.* London: Walter Scott, 1890.

Barnes, Timothy D. *Constantine and Eusebius.* Cambridge: Harvard University Press, 1981.

Bartel, Floyd G., and Richard Showalter. *A New Look at Church Growth.* Newton, Kans.: Faith and Life Press; Scottdale, Penn.: Mennonite Publishing House, 1979.

Bebb, E. Douglas. *Wesley: A Man with a Concern.* London: Epworth, 1950.

Bieler, Andre. *Architecture in Worship: The Christian Place of Worship.* Edinburgh: Oliver and Boyd, 1965.

Bouyer, Louis. *Liturgy and Architecture.* Notre Dame, Ind.: University of Notre Dame Press, 1967.

Braun, Neil. *Laity Mobilized: Reflections on Church Growth in Japan and Other Lands.* Grand Rapids: Eerdmans, 1971.

129

Calvin, John. *Institutes of the Christian Religion.* 2 vols. Edited by John T. McNeill. Translated by Ford Lewis Battles. The Library of Christian Classics, edited by John Baillie, John T. McNeill, and Henry P. Van Dusen. Philadelphia: Westminster, 1960.

Carroll, B. H. "Ecclesia, the Church." In *Studies in the New Testament Church,* edited by Louis Entzminger. Fort Worth: The Manney Company, n.d.

Chaney, Charles L. *Church Planting at the End of the Twentieth Century.* Wheaton: Tyndale House, 1982.

Chaney, Charles L., and Ron S. Lewis. *Design for Church Growth.* Nashville: Broadman, 1977.

Cho, Paul Yonggi. *The Fourth Dimension.* Plainfield, N.J.: Logos International, 1979.

———. *Solving Life's Problems.* Plainfield, N.J.: Logos International, 1980.

Cho, Paul Yonggi, with Harold Hostetler. *Successful Home Cell Groups.* Plainfield, N.J.: Logos International, 1981.

Cho, Paul Yonggi, and R. Whitney Manzano. *More Than Numbers.* Waco: Word, 1984.

Chrysostom, John. *The Homilies of St. John Chrysostom.* Oxford: John Henry Parker, 1851.

Collins, J. B. *Get a Glimpse of the World's Largest Church.* Chattanooga, Tenn.: by the author, 1973.

Conwell, Russell H. *Life of Charles Haddon Spurgeon, the World's Great Preacher.* Philadelphia: Edgewood, 1892.

Cook, Harold R. *Historic Patterns of Church Growth.* Chicago: Moody, 1971.

Criswell, W. A. *Criswell's Guidebook for Pastors.* Nashville: Broadman, 1980.

Crowfoot, J. W. *Early Churches in Palestine.* London: Oxford University Press, 1941.

Cunningham, John. *The Growth of the Church.* London: Macmillan, 1886.

Davies, J. G. *The Origin and Development of Early Christian Church Architecture.* London: SCM, 1952.

Day, Richard Ellsworth. *Rhapsody in Black: The Life Story of John Jasper.* Valley Forge: Judson, 1953.

Deissmann, Adolf. *Light from the Ancient East.* New York: Harper and Brothers, n.d.

d'Epinay, Christian Lalive. *Haven of the Masses: A Study of the Pentecostal Movement in Chile.* London: Lutterworth, 1969.

DeWolf, L. Harold. *A Theology of the Living Church.* New York: Harper and Row, 1953.

Dillistone, F. W. *The Structure of the Divine Society.* Philadelphia: Westminster, 1951.

Dix, Dom Gregory. *The Shape of the Liturgy.* London: Dacre, 1945.

Downey, Glanville. *Ancient Antioch.* Princeton: Princeton University Press, 1963.

———. *Constantinople in the Age of Justinian.* Norman, Okla.: University of Oklahoma Press, 1960.

DuBose, Francis M. *How Churches Grow in an Urban World.* Nashville: Broadman, 1978.

Duncan, Homer. *Divine Intent.* 3d rev. ed. Lubbock: The Worldwide Missionary Crusader, 1982.

Durell, J. C. V. *The Historic Church: An Essay on the Conception of the Christian Church and Its Ministry in the Sub-Apostolic Age.* 1906. New York: Kraus, 1969.

Engstrom, Ted W. *What in the World Is God Doing? The New Face of Missions.* Waco: Word, 1978.

Entzminger, Louis. *How to Organize and Administer a Great Sunday School.* Fort Worth: The Manney Company, 1949.

———, ed. *Studies in the New Testament Church.* Fort Worth: The Manney Company, n.d.

Eusebius, *The Ecclesiastical History of Eusebius Pamphilus.* Translated by Isaac Boyle. Reprint. Grand Rapids: Baker, 1955.

Falwell, Jerry, and Elmer L. Towns. Aflame. Nashville: Impact Books, 1971.

Ferguson, Everett. *Early Christians Speak.* Austin: Sweet, 1971.

Fife, Eric S., and Arthur F. Glasser. *Missions in Crisis: Rethinking Missionary Strategy.* Chicago: Inter-Varsity, 1961.

Fullerton, W. Y. *Charles Haddon Spurgeon: A Biography.* 1920. Chicago: Moody, 1966.

Gangel, Kenneth O. *Leadership for Church Education.* Chicago: Moody, 1970.

Getz, Gene A. *Sharpening the Focus of the Church.* Chicago: Moody, 1974.

Gibbs, Eddie. *I Believe in Church Growth.* Grand Rapids: Eerdmans, 1982.

Gray, Joe D. *Speak a Good Word for Jesus.* Nashville: Twentieth Century Christian, 1980.

Green, Hollis L. *Why Churches Die: A Guide to Basic Evangelism and Church Growth.* Minneapolis: Bethany Fellowship, 1972.

Green, Michael. *Called to Serve: Ministry and Ministers in the Church.* Philadelphia: Westminster, 1964.

Greenway, Roger S., ed. *Guidelines for Urban Church Planting.* Grand Rapids: Baker, 1976.

Hale, Lewis. *How Churches Can Cooperate.* Austin: Firm Foundation Publishing House, n.d.

Harkins, Paul W., trans. *St. John Chrysostom: Discourses Against Judaizing Christians.* Washington, D.C.: Catholic University of America Press, 1979.

Hatch, Edwin. *The Organization of the Early Christian Churches.* 2d rev. ed. 1888. Austin: Quality Publications, 1976.

Hawley, Monroe E. *Redigging the Wells.* Austin: Quality Publications, 1976.

Hay, Alexander R. *The New Testament Order for Church and Missionary.* Buenos Aires: SEMCA, 1947.

Hayden, Eric W. *A Centennial History of Spurgeon's Tabernacle.* Pasadena, Tex.: Pilgrim Publications, 1973.

Hayden, W. L. *Church Polity.* Chicago: S. J. Clarke, 1894.

Hayford, Jack. *The Church on the Way.* Lincoln, Va.: Chosen, 1982.

Hedley, George P. *Christian Worship: Some Meanings and Means.* New York: Macmillan, 1953.

Hesselgrave, David J. *Planting Churches Cross-Culturally: A Guide for Home and Foreign Missions.* Grand Rapids: Baker, 1980.

Hoddinott, R. F. *Early Byzantine Churches in Macedonia and Southern Serbia.* London: Macmillan, 1963.

Hodges, Melvin L. *Growing Young Churches.* Chicago: Moody, 1969.

Hoge, Dean R., and David A. Roozen, eds. *Understanding Church Growth and Decline 1950-1978.* New York: Pilgrim, 1979.

Hoover, Willis C. *Historia del Avivamiento Pentescostal en Chile.* Valparaiso: Impresa Excelsior, 1948.

Hudson, Winthrop S. "Denominationalism as a Basis for Ecumenicity: A Seventeenth Century Conception." In *Denominationalism,* edited by Russell E. Richey. Nashville: Abingdon, 1977.

Hurston, John W., and Karen L. Hurston. *Caught in the Web: The Home Cell Unit System at Full Gospel Central Church, Seoul, Korea.* Seoul: Church Growth International, 1977.

Jacobs, Jay. *Great Cathedrals.* New York: American Heritage, 1968.

Jacquet, Constant H., Jr. *Yearbook of American and Canadian Churches 1981.* Nashville: Abingdon, 1981.

Jay, Eric G. *The Church: Its Changing Image Through Twenty Centuries.* Atlanta: John Knox, 1978.

Jenson, Ron, and Jim Stevens. *Dynamics of Church Growth.* Grand Rapids: Baker, 1981.

Jones, Cheslyn, Geoffrey Wainwright, and Edward Yarnold, eds. *The Study of Liturgy.* New York: Oxford University Press, 1978.

Kennedy, Nell L. *Dream Your Way to Success: The Story of Dr. Yonggi Cho and Korea.* Plainfield, N.J.: Logos International, 1980.

Kessler, J. B. A., Jr. *A Study of the Older Protestant Missions in Peru and Chile.* Goes: Gosterbaan and le Cointre N.V., 1967.

Kidder, G. E. *The New Churches of Europe.* London: Architectural Press, 1964.

Kuen, Alfred. *I Will Build My Church.* Translated by Ruby Lindblad. Chicago: Moody, 1971.

Küng, Hans. *Structures of the Church.* Translated by Salvator Attanasio. New York: Nelson, 1964.

Lake, Kirsopp, and Foakes-Jackson, F. J., eds. *The Beginnings of Christianity.* 5 vols. Vol. 4. London: Macmillan, 1933.

Lang, G. H. *The Churches of God.* London: Paternoster, 1959.

Lightfoot, J. B. *The Apostolic Fathers.* 1891. Grand Rapids: Baker, 1956.

Luther, Martin. *Works of Martin Luther.* 6 vols. "The Papacy of Rome." Vol. 1. Philadelphia: Holman, 1930–32.

McCoy, Lee H. *Understanding Baptist Polity.* Nashville: Convention Press, 1964.

McDonald, Mary Francis. *Lactantius: The Minor Works.* "The Deaths of the Persecutors." Washington, D.C.: Catholic University of American Press, 1965.

McDowell, Mark. *How to Build a Growing, Functioning New Testament Church.* Oskaloosa, Iowa: Universal Hope Publications, 1978.

McGavran, Donald A., *How Churches Grow.* London: World Dominion, 1957.

———. *Understanding Church Growth.* Grand Rapids: Eerdmans, 1970.

McGavran, Donald A., and Winfield C. Arn. *Ten Steps for Church Growth.* San Francisco: Harper and Row, 1977.

McGavran, Donald A., with Win C. Arn. *How to Grow a Church.* Glendale, Calif.: Regal, 1973.

Machen, J. Gresham. *Christianity and Liberalism.* Grand Rapids: Eerdmans, 1923.

McQuilkin, J. Robertson. *Measuring the Church Growth Movement: Is It Biblical?* Chicago: Moody, 1974.

Mancinelli, Fabrizio. *Catacombs and Basilicas: The Early Christians in Rome.* Scala Books; distributed by Harper and Row, 1981.

Manson, T. W. *Ministry and Priesthood: Christ's and Ours.* Richmond: John Knox, 1959.

Martin, J. Henry. *John Wesley's London Chapels.* London: Epworth, 1946.

Martin, Ralph P. *Worship in the Early Church.* Grand Rapids: Eerdmans, 1964.

Martin, Roger. *R. A. Torrey: Apostle of Certainty.* Murfreesboro, Tenn.: Sword of the Lord, 1976.

Mathews, Thomas F. *The Early Churches of Constantinople: Architecture and Liturgy.* University Park: Pennsylvania State University Press, 1971.

Mead, Sidney E. "Denominationalism: The Shape of Protestantism in America." In *Denominationalism,* edited by Russell E. Richey. Nashville: Abingdon, 1977.

Moberg, David O. *The Church as a Social Institution: The Sociology of American Religion.* Englewood Cliffs, N.J.: Prentice-Hall, 1962.

Morikawa, Jitsuo. *Biblical Dimensions of Church Growth.* Valley Forge: Judson, 1979.

Morris, Leon. *Ministers of God.* London: Inter-Varsity Fellowship, 1964.

Neighbour, Ralph W., Jr., comp. *Future Church.* Nashville: Broadman, 1980.

Newman, Albert Henry. *A Manual of Church History.* 2 vols. Philadelphia: Judson, 1899.

Niebuhr, H. Richard. *The Social Sources of Denominationalism.* 1929. New York: Meridian, 1957.

Norbie, Donald L. *New Testament Church Organization.* Kansas City, Kans.: Walterick, 1977.

Olson, Gilbert W. *Church Growth in Sierra Leone: A Study of Church Growth in Africa's Oldest Protestant Mission Field.* Grand Rapids: Eerdmans, 1969.

Oosthuizen, G. C. *Moving to the Waters: Fifty Years of Pentecostal Revival in Bethesda, 1925–1975.* Durban, South Africa: Bethesda Publications, 1975.

Orjala, Paul R. *Get Ready to Grow.* Kansas City, Mo.: Beacon Hill, 1978.

Perkins, E. Benson. *Methodist Preaching Houses and the Law.* London: Epworth, 1952.

Peters, George W. *A Theology of Church Growth.* Grand Rapids: Zondervan, 1981.

Radmacher, Earl D. *What the Church Is All About: A Biblical and Historical Study.* Chicago: Moody, 1972.

Ray, David R. *Small Churches Are the Right Size.* New York: Pilgrim, 1982.

"Reaching All Power." *Reaching All.* Minneapolis: World Wide Publications, 1974.

"Reaching By All Means." *Reaching All.* Sydney, Australia: World Wide Publications, 1974.

Read, William R. *New Patterns of Church Growth in Brazil.* Grand Rapids: Eerdmans, 1965.

Read, William R., Victor M. Monterroso, and Harmon A. Johnson. *Latin American Church Growth.* Grand Rapids: Eerdmans, 1969.

Reese, Ed. *The Life and Ministry of Charles Finney.* Glenwood, Ill.: Fundamental Publishers, 1976.

——. *The Life and Ministry of DeWitt Talmage.* Glenwood, Ill.: Fundamental Publishers, 1976.

——. *The Life and Ministry of Reuben Torrey.* Glenwood, Ill.: Fundamental Publishers, 1975.

——. *The Life and Ministry of Wilbur Chapman.* Glenwood, Ill.: Fundamental Publishers, 1975.

——. *The Life and Ministry of William Riley.* Glenwood, Ill.: Fundamental Publishers, 1975.

Richey, Russell E. "The Social Sources of Denominationalism: Methodism." In *Denominationalism,* edited by Russell E. Richey. Nashville: Abingdon, 1977.

Ross, Bob L. *A Pictorial Biography of C. H. Spurgeon.* Pasadena, Tex.: Pilgrim Publications, 1974.

Russell, C. Allyn. *Voices of American Fundamentalism: Seven Biographical Studies.* Philadelphia: Westminster, 1976.

Schaller, Lyle E. *Assimilating New Members.* Nashville: Abingdon, 1978.

——. *The Multiple Staff and the Larger Church.* Nashville: Abingdon, 1980.

Scherer, Ross P., comp. *American Denominational Organization: A Sociological View.* Pasadena, Calif.: William Carey Library, 1980.

Shanks, Hershel. *Judaism in Stone.* Washington, D.C.: Biblical Archaeology Society: New York: Harper and Row, 1979.

Sine, Tom. *The Mustard Seed Conspiracy: You Can Make a Difference in Tomorrow's Troubled World.* Waco: Word, 1981.

Snyder, Howard A. *The Community of the King.* Downers Grove: Inter-Varsity, 1977.

———. *The Problem of Wine Skins: Church Structure in a Technological Age.* Downers Grove: Inter-Varsity, 1975.

———. *The Radical Wesley and Patterns for Church Renewal.* Downers Grove: Inter-Varsity, 1980.

Stanley, Arthur P. *The Epistles of St. Paul to the Corinthians.* London: John Murray, 1882.

Strong, Augustus H. *Systematic Theology.* 1907. Philadelphia: Judson, 1947.

Stroop, J. Ridley. *The Church of the Bible.* Nashville: J. Ridley Stroop, 1962.

Sullivan, James L. *Baptist Polity as I See It.* Nashville: Broadman, 1983.

Swindoll, Charles R. *Dropping Your Guard: The Value of Open Relations.* Waco: Word, 1983.

Taylor, E. L. Hebden. *Reformation or Revolution: A Study of Modern Society in the Light of a Reformational and Scriptural Pluralism.* Nutley, N.J.: Craig, 1970.

Thiessen, Henry Clarence. *Introductory Lectures in Systematic Theology.* Grand Rapids: Eerdmans, 1949.

Tillapaugh, Frank R. *The Church Unleashed: Getting God's People Out Where the Needs Are.* Ventura, Calif.: Regal, 1982.

Tippett, Alan R. *Church Growth and the Word of God.* Grand Rapids: Eerdmans, 1970.

Towns, Elmer L. *America's Fastest Growing Churches: Why Ten Sunday Schools Are Growing Fast.* Nashville: Impact Books, 1972.

———. *Getting a Church Started.* Lynchburg, Va.: by the author, Liberty Graduate School of Religion, 1982.

———. *Is the Day of the Denomination Dead?* Nashville: Nelson, 1973.

———. *The Successful Sunday School and Teachers Guidebook.* Carol Stream, Ill.: Creation House, 1976.

———. *The Ten Largest Sunday Schools and What Makes Them Grow.* Grand Rapids: Baker, 1960.

Towns, Elmer L., John N. Vaughan, and David J. Seifert. *The Complete Book of Church Growth.* Wheaton: Tyndale House, 1981.

Troeltsch, Ernst. *The Social Teaching of the Christian Churches.* Translated by Olive Wyan. London: George Allen and Unwin, 1931.

Turnbull, Ralph G. *A History of Preaching.* Grand Rapids: Baker, 1974.

Vajta, Vilmos, ed. *The Gospel and the Ambiguity of the Church.* Philadelphia: Fortress, 1974.

Wagner, C. Peter. *Church Growth and the Whole Gospel: A Biblical Mandate.* San Francisco: Harper and Row, 1981.

———. *Frontiers in Missionary Strategy.* Chicago: Moody, 1971.

———. *Leading Your Church to Growth.* Ventura, Calif.: Regal, 1984.

———. *Look Out! The Pentecostals Are Coming.* Carol Stream, Ill.: Creation House, 1973.

———. *Our Kind of People: The Ethical Dimensions of Church Growth in America.* Atlanta: John Knox, 1979.

———. *Stop the World, I Want to Get On.* Glendale, Calif.: Regal, 1974.

———. *Your Church Can Grow.* Glendale, Calif.: Regal, 1976.

Ward, J. W. C. *A History of the Early Church to A.D. 500.* London: Methuen, 1937.

Weber, Max. *The Theory of Social and Economic Organization.* Edited by Talcott Parsons. Translated by A. M. Henderson. New York: Oxford University Press, 1947.

Werning, Waldo J. *Vision and Strategy for Church Growth.* Chicago: Moody, 1977.

Westin, Gunnar. *The Free Church Through the Ages.* Translated by Virgil A. Olson. Nashville: Broadman, 1958.

White, Jerry. *The Church and the Parachurch: An Uneasy Marriage.* Portland: Multnomah, 1983.

Willems, Emilio. *Followers of the New Faith: Culture Change and the Rise of Protestantism in Brazil and Chile.* Nashville: Vanderbilt University Press, 1967.

Womack, David A. *Breaking the Stained-Glass Barrier.* New York: Harper and Row, 1973.

Yeakley, Flavil R., Jr. *Church Leadership and Organization.* Arvada, Colo.: Christian Communications, 1980.

## Periodicals

Alexander, Gary. "House Churches Your Hope for the Future?" *Christian Life,* January 1982, pp. 32–34, 43–44.

*Baptist and Reflector,* 3 November 1982, p. 16.

*The Baptist Program,* March 1981, pp. 9, 11.

Bendix, Reinhard. "Reflections of Charismatic Leadership." *Asian Survey,* June 1967, p. 307.

Bohr, P. Richard. "State Religion in China Today: Christianity's Future in a Marxist Setting." *Missiology,* July 1983, p. 329.

"Building 'Bridges' in Russia." *Worldwide Challenge,* April 1978, pp. 37–38.

Castro, Emilio. "Pentecostalism and Ecumenism in Latin America." *Christianity Today,* 29 September 1972, p. 995.

Chaney, Charles L. "A New Day for New Churches." *Church Growth Bulletin,* March 1976, pp. 512–16.

*Church Growth Bulletin,* November 1975, p. 491.

"Church Growth Calculations: Facts and Fallacies, No. 1." *Church Growth Bulletin,* March 1970, p. 59.

Corvin, R. O. "Gloria a Dios: World's Largest Pentecostal Sanctuary Dedicated." *The Pentecostal Holiness Advocate,* 9 February 1975, pp. 4–5.

Davis, James. "Charisma in the 1952 Campaign." *American Political Science Review*, December 1954, p. 1085.

Fagen, Richard. "Charismatic Authority and the Leadership of Fidel Castro." *Western Political Quarterly*, January 1965, p. 275.

Friendrich, Carl. "Political Leadership and the Problem of Charismatic Power." *Journal of Politics*, February 1961, p. 26.

Gerber, Virgil. "A New Tool for Winning the City." *Church Growth Bulletin*, July 1976, pp. 542-44.

Glasser, Arthur F. "Timeless Lessons from the Western Missionary Penetration of China." *Missiology*, October 1973, pp. 455-56.

Harper, Michael. "Duplicating the New Testament Church: What Organizational Chart Does Scripture Give? *Eternity*, April 1978, pp. 24-25, 37.

Hunter, George. "Can Methodism Recover Evangelism?" *Church Growth Bulletin*, February 1977, pp. 109-18.

"Is Evangelical Theology Changing?" *Christian Life*, March 1956, pp. 16-19.

Kessler, J. B. A., Jr. "Hindrances to Church Growth." *International Review of Missions*, July 1968, p. 301.

King, Louis L. "A Rising Tide of Expectation." *Church Growth Bulletin*, September 1979, pp. 291-92.

Larkin, William J. "Matthews—Tall Pines of the Sierra." *Moody Monthly*, November 1974, pp. 83-86.

MacDonald, Gordon. "Ten Conditions for Church Growth." *Leadership*, Winter 1983, pp. 44-48.

Miranda, Juan Carlos. "'Rosario' Came Just in Time." *Church Growth Bulletin*, September 1977, pp. 150-51.

Montgomery, James H., interviewer. "Church Growth Flourishes in America." *Church Growth Bulletin*, November 1976, pp. 86-89.

O'Connor, Edward D. "Evangelical Leaders Assess Home Churches." *Christian Life*, 1 January 1982, p. 32.

Patterson, George. "Multiply Churches Through Extension Chains." *Church Growth Bulletin*, July 1974.

Petersen, J. Randall. "Church Growth: A Limitation of Numbers?" *Christianity Today*, 27 March 1981, pp. 406-11.

Rickard, Marvin G. "Church Planting—It Can Be Exciting." *Christian Life*, January 1982, pp. 48-49.

Rutland, John. "Riotous Times Spawned University Church, Manila." *Baptist Standard*, 27 July 1983, p. 9.

"Six Churches: Thriving on Common Ground." *Christianity Today*, 21 May 1976, pp. 24-25.

Synder, Howard A. "'The People of God'—Implications for Church Structure." *Christianity Today*, 27 October 1972, pp. 6-11.

Stetz, John, and Jim Montgomery. "Biggest Little Church in the World." *Christian Life*, February 1977, pp. 58, 60–61.

Synan, Vinson. "Mission to Chile." *The International Pentecostal Holiness Advocate*, 13 July 1980, pp. 4–5.

Towns, Elmer L. "Big Churches: Yes!" *Christianity Today*, 5 November 1971, p. 8.

———. "The Case for the Large Sunday School." *Christian Life*, March 1971, p. 58.

———. "The Small, Personal Sunday School." *Christian Life*, April 1971, pp. 48–49.

———. "What Makes Large Sunday Schools Larger?" *Christian Life*, December 1972, p. 70.

Tucker, Robert. "The Theory of Charismatic Leadership." *Daedalus*, Summer 1968, p. 747.

Wagner, C. Peter. "Aiming at Church Growth in the Eighties." *Christianity Today*, 21 November 1980, p. 27.

———. "American Church Growth Update." *United Evangelical Action*, Spring 1974, p. 39.

———. "The Street 'Seminaries' of Chile." *Christianity Today*, 6 August 1971, pp. 5–8.

———. "What Makes a Church Grow?" *United Evangelical Action*, June 1974, pp. 55–56.

Wagner, C. Peter, and Richard L. Gorsuch. "The Quality Church (Part 1)." *Leadership*, Winter 1983, pp. 28–32.

Walvoord, John F. "Evangelical Leaders Assess Home Churches." *Christian Life*, 1 January 1982, p. 32.

Ward, Larry. "Dr. Han Kyung Chik, Korea's Quiet Dynamo." *World Vision*, March 1968, p. 18.

Wenhan, Jiang. "The Present Situation of Christianity in China." *Missiology*, July 1983, pp. 259–65.

Williams, Sherman. "Mothering Churches." *United Evangelical Action*, Summer 1977, pp. 22–24, 34.

Willner, Ann, and Dorothy Willner. "The Rise and Role of Charismatic Leaders." *Annals of the American Academy of Political and Social Science*, March 1965, pp. 61–69.

## Unpublished Materials

### Correspondence

Slocumb, Douglas W. Letter to author. 5 February 1982. Church of God World Misions, Cleveland, Tennessee.

Thompson, Alex. Letter to author. 15 March 1983. Full Gospel Church of God in South Africa, Durban.

### Dissertations

Bitner, James Henry. "A Critical Study of Baptist Church Growth in Chile." Ph.D. diss., Southwestern Baptist Theological Seminary, Fort Worth, February 1975.

Faulkner, Randall. "The Branch Church Ministry: An Innovation in Church Growth Strategy." D.Min. diss., Trinity Evangelical Divinity School, Deerfield, Illinois, 1984.

### Research Paper

Sanchez, Daniel. "Viable Models for Churches in Communities Experiencing Ethnic Transition." Fuller Theological Seminary, Pasadena, 1979.

### Questionnaire

Smith, Chuck. Questionnaire for *The World's Twenty Largest Churches*. 2 August 1983. Calvary Chapel, Santa Ana, California.

## Other Sources

### Interviews

Faulkner, J. R. July 1983. Highland Park Baptist Church, Chattanooga, Tennessee.

International Church of the Four Square Gospel, Los Angeles. 8 June 1983.

Jones, Don. 20 January 1984. Korean Baptist Mission, Seoul.

Rawlings, Harold. June 1983. Landmark Baptist Temple, Cincinnati.

# *Index*